Concurring Opinion Writing on the U.S. Supreme Court

SUNY series in American Constitutionalism

Robert J. Spitzer, editor

Concurring Opinion Writing on the U.S. Supreme Court

PAMELA C. CORLEY

Published by
State University of New York Press, Albany

© 2010 State University of New York

All rights reserved

Printed in the United States of America

No part of this book may be used or reproduced in any manner whatsoever without written permission. No part of this book may be stored in a retrieval system or transmitted in any form or by any means including electronic, electrostatic, magnetic tape, mechanical, photocopying, recording, or otherwise without the prior permission in writing of the publisher.

For information, contact State University of New York Press, Albany, NY
www.sunypress.edu

Production by Ryan Morris
Marketing by Anne M. Valentine

Library of Congress Cataloging-in-Publication Data

Corley, Pamela C., 1967–
    Concurring opinion writing on the U.S. Supreme Court / Pamela C. Corley.
      p. cm. — (SUNY series in American constitutionalism)
    Includes bibliographical references and index.
    ISBN 978-1-4384-3067-6 (hardcover : alk. paper)
    ISBN 978-1-4384-3066-9 (pbk. : alk. paper)
    1. United States. Supreme Court. 2. Concurring opinions—United States. 3. Judicial process—United States I. Title.

KF8742.C67 2010
347.73'26—dc22
                                      2009023198

10 9 8 7 6 5 4 3 2 1

To my husband Greg and my daughter Megan

Contents

List of Illustrations		ix
Acknowledgments		xi
Chapter 1:	Introduction	1
Chapter 2:	Why Justices Write or Join: Modeling Concurring Behavior	21
Chapter 3:	Potential Concurrences: Insight from Justices Blackmun and Marshall	41
Chapter 4:	The Impact of Concurring Opinions	71
Chapter 5:	Conclusion	95
Appendix		101
Notes		121
References		129
Table of Cases		139
Index		141

Illustrations

Figures

1.1	Proportion of Cases with at Least One Concurrence Versus Proportion of Cases with at Least One Dissent	8
2.1	Proportion of Cases with Concurring and Dissenting Opinions, 1937–2004 Terms	22

Tables

1.1.	Proportion of Cases with at Least One Concurrence Versus Proportion of Cases with at Least One Dissent	9
2.1.	Summary of Hypotheses	30
2.2.	Types of Concurrences, by Justice (1986–1989)	32
2.3.	Results of Concurrence Model	34
2.4.	Predicted Probabilities of Justices' Decisions to Write or Join a Specific Type of Concurrence Versus Joining the Majority Opinion (1986–1989)	36
3.1.	Bargaining and Accommodation Between Blackmun and Marshall and the other Justices, 1986–1989 Terms	45
4.1.	Distribution of the Types of Concurrences: Supreme Court Versus Courts of Appeals	83
4.2.	Summary of Model of Impact of Concurrences on Lower Court Compliance	84
4.3.	Predicted Probabilities of Positive Treatment by the Lower Courts	85

4.4.	Summary of Model of Impact of Multiple Concurrences on Lower Court Compliance	88
4.5.	Summary of the Impact of the Type of Concurrence on the Supreme Court's Positive Treatment of its Own Precedent	91
4.6.	Predicted Probabilities of Positive Treatment by the Supreme Court	92
A.1.	List of Cases, the Type of Concurrence, and the Justice Writing the Concurrence	101
A.2.	Multinomial Logit Model of Justices' Decisions to Write or Join a Specific Type of Concurrence Versus Joining the Majority Decision (1986–1989 Terms)	113
A.3.	Descriptive Statistics for Independent Variables in Multinomial Logit Model of Justices' Decisions to Write or Join a Specific Type of Concurrence Versus Joining the Majority Decision (1986–1989 Terms)	114
A.4.	Logit Model of the Impact of Concurrences on Treatment of Supreme Court Precedent in the Courts of Appeals	114
A.5.	Descriptive Statistics for Independent Variables in Logit Model of the Impact of Concurrences on Treatment of Supreme Court Precedent in the Courts of Appeals	115
A.6.	Logit Model of the Impact of Multiple Concurrences on Treatment of Supreme Court Precedent in the Courts of Appeals	116
A.7.	Predicted Probabilities of Positive Treatment, by Circuit	117
A.8.	Logit Model of the Impact of Type of Concurrence on Positive Treatment of Supreme Court Precedent by the Supreme Court	118
A.9.	Descriptive Statistics for Independent Variables in Logit Model of the Impact of the Type of Concurrence on Positive Treatment of Supreme Court Precedent by the Supreme Court	119

Acknowledgments

In writing this book I received a great deal of help and I would like to acknowledge those whose support made this project possible. First, I thank Bob Howard. Without his guidance and support I would not have completed this project. He was an incredible mentor when I was a graduate student and he still continues in that role. I also thank Dave Nixon and Scott Graves, both of whom provided a great deal of assistance in the beginning stages of this project.

I am also grateful to a number of scholars for their advice and comments. I am particularly grateful to Larry Baum, Paul Collins, Christian Grose, Suzanne Globetti, Marc Hetherington, Stefanie Lindquist, Kirk Randazzo, Neal Tate, and Chris Zorn. Special thanks to Art Ward for reading the entire manuscript and offering invaluable suggestions. For their research assistance, I thank Camille Burge, Sarah Hinde, Gbemende Johnson, Jennifer Selin, and Jenna Lukasik. I also thank Steve Wermiel, who has always given me support and encouragement.

Early versions of this research were presented at the annual meetings of the Midwest Political Science Association (2004, 2006) and the Southern Political Science Association (2005, 2006). Special thanks go to the many colleagues who offered comments and suggestions. Additionally, an earlier version of Chapter 3 was published as "Bargaining and Accommodation on the United States Supreme Court: Insight from Justice Blackmun" in *Judicature* (90, pp. 157–65, January–February 2007).

Finally, I thank my husband Greg and my daughter Megan, to whom I am grateful for their love and support.

1

Introduction

During his introductory remarks at Judge Samuel Alito's Supreme Court confirmation hearings, Senate Judiciary Committee Chairman Arlen Specter referred to Justice Robert H. Jackson's concurrence in *Youngstown Sheet & Tube Co. v. Sawyer* (1952):

> This hearing comes at a time of great national concern about the balance between civil rights and the president's national security authority. The president's constitutional powers as commander in chief to conduct electronic surveillance appear to conflict with what Congress has said in the Foreign Intelligence Surveillance Act. This conflict involves very major considerations raised by Justice Jackson's historic concurrence in the Youngstown Steel seizure cases ... where [he] noted, quote, "What is at stake is the equilibrium established in our constitutional system." (Specter 2006)

Jackson's concurrence has been called "the greatest single opinion ever written by a Supreme Court justice" (Levinson 2000), establishing the starting framework for analyzing all future foreign relations and individual liberties problems.

Youngstown involved a labor dispute in the steel industry during the Korean War. President Harry S. Truman issued an executive order directing the secretary of commerce to seize the steel mills and keep them operating. Truman argued this was a necessary action to prevent "a national catastrophe which would inevitably result from a stoppage of steel production" (582). The Court overturned the order, holding that presidential authority "must stem either from an act of Congress or the Constitution itself" (585). According to the Court, the Commander in Chief Clause does not give the president "ultimate power" to "take possession of private property in order to keep labor disputes from stopping production" (587). That power belongs only to Congress.

In his concurrence, Jackson contended that the president's powers "are not fixed but fluctuate, depending on their disjunction or conjunction with those of Congress" (*Youngstown* 1952, 635). He conceived of three categories:

1. Where the president acts pursuant to express or implied authorization of Congress, in which case his authority is at its maximum;

2. Where the president acts in the absence of either a congressional grant or denial of authority, in which case "there is a zone of twilight in which he and Congress may have concurrent authority, or in which its distribution is uncertain" (637); and

3. Where the president acts adversely to the express or implied will of Congress, in which case his power is "at its lowest ebb" (637).

Jackson's concurrence has been widely relied on in later decisions (Paulsen 2002). For example, *Dames & Moore v. Regan* (1981) involved Jimmy Carter's response to the taking of American hostages in Iran. The Court relied on Jackson's tripartite framework to uphold President Carter's power to order the transfer of Iranian assets out of the country, to nullify attachments of those assets, and to require that claims would be settled by arbitration rather than by U.S. courts. The Court quoted Jackson's concurrence, stating "[b]ecause the President's action in nullifying the attachments and ordering the transfer of the assets was taken pursuant to specific congressional authorization, it is 'supported by the strongest of presumptions and the widest latitude of judicial interpretation'" (674).

The lasting impact of Jackson's concurring opinion underscores the potential importance of concurrences. Why are they written? What systematic impact do these opinions have? A concurring opinion is one written by a judge or justice, in which he or she agrees with the conclusions or results of the majority opinion filed in the case "though he states separately his views of the case or his reasons for so concurring" (Black 1991, 200). When justices write or join a concurring opinion, they demonstrate that they have preferences over legal rules and they are responding to the substance of the majority opinion. Concurrences provide a way for the justices to express their views about the law, and to engage in a dialogue of law with each other, the legal community, the public, and Congress. "[C]oncurring voices produce the legal debate that furthers the intellectual development of the law on the Supreme Court" (Maveety 2005, 139). By studying the process of opinion writing and the formation of legal doctrine through focusing on concurrences, this book provides a richer and more complete portrait of judicial decision making. First, I code concurring opinions into different categories and examine why a justice writes or joins a particular type of concurrence rather than silently joining the majority opinion. Second, I provide a qualitative analysis of the bargaining and accommodation that occurs on the Supreme Court in order to further understand why concurrences are published. Finally, I assess the impact that concurring opinions have on lower court compliance and on the Supreme Court's interpretation of its own precedent.

Court Opinions Matter

Legal scholars study the opinions of the Court, dissecting the language in an effort to understand the law. Practitioners analyze and study the content of Court opinions in order to provide legal advice to their clients, using cases to predict what courts will do in a specific case that has yet to come before them. It is the rationale used in the past that provides the guidance for the future. Thus, the words used, the reasoning employed, the rationale given, and the tests devised by the Court, are important to understand. Where do they come from? How do judges agree on the language used in opinions?

There has been a long-standing debate about how researchers should study judicial behavior. Attitudinalists[1] argue that the best way to understand how judges make decisions is through a scientific, empirical approach, focusing on case outcomes and specifically on the votes of individual justices (see, e.g., Schubert 1959; Spaeth 1965; Ulmer 1959). Legally oriented scholars suggest that, in order to understand judicial behavior, we must study the language of opinions (see, e.g., Mendelson 1963). Although there continues to be disagreement, many judicial scholars have recognized the real-world importance of the content of Supreme Court opinions.

> The Opinion of the Court is the core of the policy-making power of the Supreme Court. The vote on the merits in conference determines only whether the decisions of the court below will be affirmed or reversed. It is the majority opinion which lays down the broad constitutional and legal principles that govern the decision in the case before the Court, which are theoretically binding on lower courts in all similar cases, and which establish precedents for future decisions of the Court. (Rohde and Spaeth 1976, 172)

Thus, court *opinions* matter, not just the vote on the merits, and understanding how the opinion writing process works is central to explaining the development of the law. How is legal precedent formed? How are Supreme Court opinions developed? These are questions that have become central to judicial scholars.

Previous literature has focused on explaining case outcomes or the behavior of individual justices (see, e.g., Pritchett 1948; Rohde and Spaeth 1976; Schubert 1965; Segal and Cover 1989; Segal and Spaeth 1993, 2002). According to the attitudinal model, judicial outcomes reflect a combination of legal facts and the policy preferences of individual justices. "Simply put, Rehnquist vote[d] the way he [did] because he [was] extremely conservative; Marshall voted the way he did because he [was] extremely liberal" (Segal and Spaeth 1993, 65). In short, ideology matters. However, the empirical evidence is based on the justice's final vote on the merits; thus it does not explain how opinions are crafted. In fact, Spaeth (1995) observed, "opinion coalitions and opinion writing may be a matter where nonattitudinal variables operate" (314).

With this in mind, recent literature has focused on examining the factors that shape Court opinions (see, e.g., Epstein and Knight 1998; Maltzman, Spriggs, and Wahlbeck 2000). These proponents of the strategic model have shown that preferences alone do not account for the choices that justices make. "Instead, their decisions result from the pursuit of their policy preferences within constraints endogenous to the Court. These constraints primarily stem from institutional rules on the Court, which give the Court its collegial character" (Maltzman et al. 2000, 149). In other words, although the justices want to maximize their policy preferences and see those policy preferences reflected in the law, they are *not* unconstrained. "Rather, justices are strategic actors who realize that their ability to achieve their goals depends on a consideration of the preferences of other actors, the choices they expect others to make, and the institutional context in which they act" (Epstein and Knight 1998, 10). For example, the opinion writing process on the Court is affected by the informal rule that Court opinions constitute precedent only when supported by a majority of the justices. This means that the justices, when writing the majority opinion, have to take into account the preferences of their colleagues and cannot write the opinion solely for themselves.

Scholars have studied the assignment of the majority opinion, the writing of the majority opinion, the justices' choice of what bargaining tactics to use, and the decision of each justice to join the majority decision. However, the final goal has not been achieved: "explaining the actual content of Court opinions" (Maltzman et al. 2000, 154). This is the challenge I take up in this book, specifically by focusing on concurring opinions.

Concurrences versus Dissents

After the Court hears oral arguments, it meets in private to discuss the cases and to vote. Under Court norms, if the chief justice is in the majority, he assigns the opinion. If the chief is not in the majority, the senior justice in the majority assigns the opinion. After the opinion is assigned, the majority opinion author writes a first draft, which is then circulated to the other justices.

During the opinion writing process, a justice has various options. First, the justice can join the opinion. This means he agrees with the majority opinion and does not want any changes. Second, the justice can ask the opinion writer to make changes to the opinion, bargaining with the opinion writer over specific language contained in the draft. Third, the justice can write or join a regular concurrence, which is a concurrence agreeing with the result and with the content of the opinion. Fourth, a justice can write or join a special concurrence, which is a concurrence that agrees with the result, but does not agree with the rationale used by the majority opinion writer. Fifth, the justice can write or join a dissent.

In this book, I focus solely on concurrences because concurring opinions raise a theoretical puzzle for scholars of the Supreme Court and provide a unique opportunity to differentiate between voting for the outcome versus voting for the opinion. Because concurring opinion writers agree with who wins the case, yet are still not satisfied with the legal rule announced in the opinion, concurring opinions are more difficult to understand than dissents. Dissents disagree with both the outcome and the legal reasoning of the majority opinion, and previous research shows dissents are primarily the result of ideology, specifically the ideological distance between the justice and the majority opinion writer (see Wahlbeck, Spriggs, and Maltzman 1999). On the other hand, when a justice writes or joins a concurring opinion, one asks: "Why undermine the policy voice of a majority one supports by filing a concurrence?" (Maveety 2005, 138).

Additionally, concurrences have more authority than dissents. In fact, the rules and policies of the case may be less the result of what the majority opinion holds than the interpretation of the opinion by concurring justices (see Maveety 2005). Moreover, a Court opinion is not necessarily "perceived ... as a discrete resolution of a single matter but as one link in a chain of developing law" (Ray 1990, 830). Thus, the concurrences bracketing the majority opinion may shape the evolution of the law as they limit, expand, clarify, or contradict the Court opinion.

Concurrences and Judicial Signaling

To effectuate the rule of law, one must be able to identify controlling legal principles. Furthermore, because few Supreme Court cases can answer all questions about an issue, lower court judges must interpret the decision in order to apply it. In *Roe v. Wade* (1973), the Court held that the right to privacy included a woman's right to choose whether or not to have an abortion, but did not address spousal consent, parental consent, or Medicaid funding. Thus, lower courts had to interpret *Roe* to apply it to these situations. Obviously, the majority opinion itself can communicate to the lower courts how to apply the rules, tests, and general principles contained in the opinion, and, in fact, "[p]art of the precedential system is the signaling function to lower courts" (Berkolow 2008, 303).[2] Former Chief Justice Rehnquist argued that "an appellate judge's primary task is to function as a member of a collegial body which must decide important questions of federal law in a way that gives intelligible guidance to the bench" (Rehnquist 1992, 270). However, sometimes the Court deliberately leaves legal questions open, with the intention of resolving them in future cases. Other times, the controlling legal principle is difficult if not impossible to extract from the majority opinion. When justices write or join concurring opinions, they are often revealing their support and understanding of the majority opinion and their preferences regarding the particular legal issue. "[A] concurring author ... offers an internal commentary on the court's judgment, throwing partial illumination on the otherwise obscure process that creates majorities" (Ray 1990, 783).

Based on the foregoing, I argue that concurrences are a form of judicial signaling, where judges use the signals contained in concurring opinions to interpret the majority opinion and apply it to the case before them.

This idea of judicial signaling is closely tied to the Supreme Court agenda setting literature. Scholars have emphasized the extent to which the work of the justices can be understood as "cues" or "signals" to outside actors as to the Court's interests and the possible direction that it wishes to take the law (see Baird 2007; Pacelle 1991; Perry 1991). Concurrences are the perfect vehicle for sending cues to other actors because concurring opinions are not the product of compromise as are majority opinions. A justice writing or joining a concurrence can explain "with greater precision [his] relationship to a majority opinion or holding" (Ray 1990, 829). A concurring opinion writer may signal to the other justices and the legal community the extent to which he agrees with the rationale of the majority opinion and how much support he may give in the future. For example, in *Morse v. Frederick* (2007), the Court addressed whether a school principal may, consistent with the First Amendment, restrict student speech at a school event when that speech is reasonably viewed as promoting illegal drug use. In *Morse*, a student was suspended from school for displaying a banner reading "Bong Hits 4 Jesus" across the street from his school during the Olympics torch relay. Chief Justice Roberts, writing for the majority, concluded that the principal did not violate the First Amendment by confiscating the pro-drug banner and suspending the student responsible for it. The majority found that Frederick's "Bong Hits" banner was displayed during a school event, which made this a "school speech" case rather than a normal speech case.[3]

Although the Court concluded that the banner's message was "cryptic," it was undeniably a "reference to illegal drugs" and it was reasonable for the principal to believe that it "advocated the use of illegal drugs."

Justice Thomas wrote a concurrence, arguing that students in public schools do not have a right to free speech and that *Tinker v. Des Moines Community School Dist.* (1969), a case in which the Court held that students do not "shed their constitutional rights to freedom of speech or expression at the schoolhouse gate" (506) should be overruled.[4] Basically, Thomas did not believe the majority decision went far enough and signaled his willingness to overrule *Tinker* and his belief that the First Amendment does not protect student speech in public schools. He was quite transparent in his concurrence, specifically stating that he "join[s] the Court's opinion because it erodes *Tinker's* hold in the realm of student speech, even though it does so by adding to the patchwork of exceptions to the *Tinker* standard. I think the better approach is to dispense with *Tinker* altogether, and given the opportunity, I would do so" (*Morse* 2007, 2636).

Justice Alito, joined by Justice Kennedy, wrote a concurrence agreeing with the majority opinion, but communicated his understanding that the opinion "goes no further than to hold that a public school may restrict speech that a reasonable observer would interpret as advocating illegal drug use" and that "it provides no support for any restriction of speech that can plausibly be interpreted as commenting on any political or social issue" (2636). Thus, Alito and Kennedy signaled the limited holding of the majority opinion, specifically that they would not be willing to extend the reasoning of the case to situations in which the speech could be classified as political or social speech.

In this scenario, the lower courts must interpret the majority opinion, and, in addition to reading and analyzing the majority opinion, they may also rely on the two concurring opinions in order to understand how to apply *Morse* to the case before them. The two concurrences communicate the parameters of the Court's opinion, the desired take on the majority opinion they are joining, and the preferences of the justices. These concurrences highlight the difference between voting for the *result* and voting for the *opinion*. One scholar argues:

> [J]ustices care most about the underlying legal principles in an opinion, rather than just which side wins the case. The justices want legal policy to reflect their policy preferences because they understand that it is those policies that ultimately influence distributional consequences in society. It is the legal rule announced in an opinion (not which party won the case) that ultimately serves as referents for behavior and alters the perceived costs and

benefits decision makers attach to alternative courses of action. (Spriggs 2003)

Concurrences provide justices with discretionary opportunities to voice their legal perspectives, and, although there are opportunity costs involved with writing a concurring opinion, justices increasingly choose to write them in the modern era. Table 1.1 presents the proportion of cases with at least one concurrence versus the proportion of cases with at least one dissent for the Warren, Burger, and Rehnquist Courts and Figure 1.1 displays this information graphically. During the Warren Court, the proportion of cases with at least one concurrence was .317 and the proportion of cases with at least one dissent was .631. During the Burger Court, the proportion of cases with at least one concurrence jumped to .436 and then went down slightly during the Rehnquist Court to .427. During the Burger Court, the proportion of cases with at least one dissent was .638, whereas the proportion of cases with at least one dissent went down to .586 during the Rehnquist Court.

Why does a justice write or join a concurring opinion rather than silently joining the majority? What factors influence this decision? What do concurrences tell us about the opinion writing process on the Supreme Court? What do they tell us about the bargaining and accommodation that occurs? Do published concurring opinions have an impact on lower court

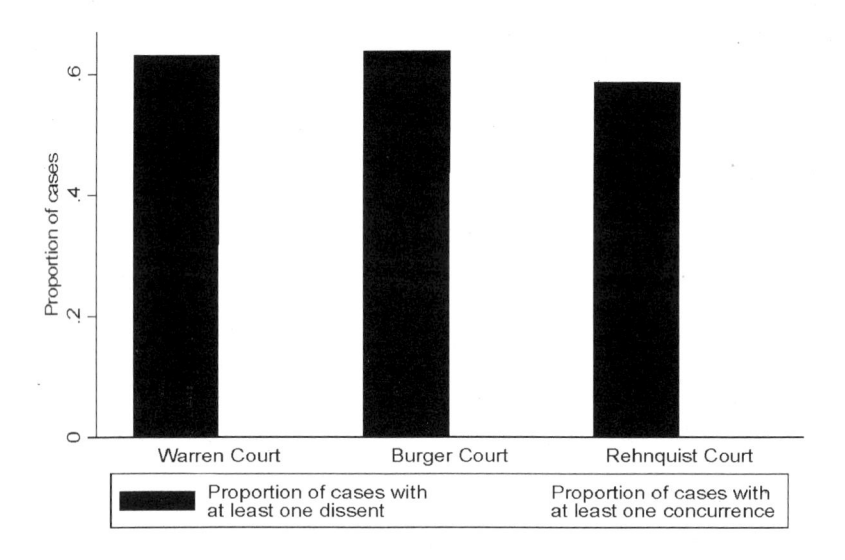

Figure 1.1. Proportion of Cases with at Least One Concurrence Versus Proportion of Cases with at Least One Dissent.

Table 1.1. Proportion of Cases with at Least One Concurrence Versus Proportion of Cases with at Least One Dissent

Court	Total number of cases	Number of cases with concurring opinions	Proportion of cases with at least one concurrence	Number of cases with dissenting opinions	Proportion of cases with at least one dissent
Warren	1,792	568	.317	1,131	.631
Burger	2,404	1,048	.436	1,533	.638
Rehnquist	1,860	794	.427	1,090	.586

Note: The Rehnquist Court numbers are through the 2004 term.

compliance and even the Supreme Court itself? I address each of these questions in the following chapters.

The Importance of Concurrences

Concurring opinions are important for many reasons. First, a concurrence can transform a majority opinion into a plurality. A plurality opinion is one in which a majority of the Court agrees to the result, but less than a majority of the justices agree to the reasons behind the decision. The plurality opinion generally is regarded as a source of uncertainty and instability in the law, creating confusion in lower courts that are bound to follow the precedent established by the Supreme Court. In fact, scholars argue that plurality opinions disrupt the signaling function to lower courts (see Berkolow 2008) and, in fact, one study shows that lower courts are less likely to comply with Supreme Court plurality opinions than majority opinions (Corley 2009). Thus, understanding how concurrences develop and why they are written is crucial to understanding how the rule of law develops, since rule-of-law values require that individuals be able to identify controlling legal principles.

Second, concurring opinions may undermine the force of a unanimous Court. The Court recognized the importance of a unified response in *Brown v. Board of Education* (1954), a case in which the Supreme Court held that racial segregation in public schools was unconstitutional. In *Brown*, Chief Justice Warren wished to avoid concurring opinions. "He wanted a single, unequivocating opinion that could leave no doubt that the Court had put Jim Crow to the sword" (Kluger 1977, 683). Scholars have argued that a decision accompanied by a concurrence speaks with less authority than a single unanimous opinion (see Ray 1990) and a recent study found that cases with a larger number of concurring opinions are more likely than other cases to be overruled by the Supreme Court in the future (Spriggs and Hansford 2001).

A third reason concurring opinions are important is that they may contribute to the development of the law. An example is Justice O'Connor's concurrence in *Lynch v. Donnelly* (1984). In *Lynch*, the Court found that a city's Christmas display, which included reindeer, a Christmas tree, colored lights, a season's greeting banner, and a nativity scene, did not violate the Establishment Clause.[5] In reaching its decision, the Court applied a three-prong test, called the *Lemon* test,[6] finding that the city had a secular purpose for the display, the primary effect was not to advance religion, and that there was no undue administrative entanglement. Justice O'Connor joined the majority, but wrote a separate concurrence criticizing the Court's reliance on *Lemon*. She proposed a new test, the "endorsement test," to replace the purpose and effect prong of the *Lemon* test by asking "whether the government intends to convey a message of endorsement or disapproval of religion" and whether the practice in question has the "effect of communicating a message of government endorsement or disapproval of religion." Later, in *County of Allegheny v. American Civil Liberties Union* (1989), the Court used O'Connor's endorsement test, finding that the display of a crèche inside a county courthouse violated the Establishment Clause because it had "the effect of promoting or endorsing religious beliefs."

Fourth, a concurring opinion can improve the majority opinion. "[H]uman nature being what it is, nothing causes the writer to be as solicitous of objections on major points as the knowledge that, if he does not accommodate them, he will not have a unanimous court, and will have to confront a separate concurrence" (Scalia 1994, 41). According to Justice Scalia:

> The dissent or concurrence puts my opinion to the test, providing a direct confrontation of the best arguments on both sides of the disputed points. It is a sure cure for laziness, compelling me to make the most of my case. Ironic as it may seem, I think a higher percentage of the worst opinions of my Court—not in result but in reasoning—are unanimous ones. (Scalia 1994, 41)

Justice Ginsburg agrees with Scalia, arguing that "[t]he prospect of a . . . separate concurring statement pointing out an opinion's inaccuracies and inadequacies strengthens the test; it heightens the opinion writer's incentive to 'get it right'" (Ginsburg 1990, 139).

Furthermore, some argue that concurrences reflect democratic values. "[D]isagreement among judges is as true to the character of democracy, and as vital, as freedom of speech itself. . . . Indeed, we may remind ourselves, unanimity in the law is possible only in fascist and communist countries" (Fuld 1962, 926). Thomas Jefferson complained about unanimous opinions "huddled up in conclave, perhaps by a majority of one, delivered as if unanimous, and with the silent acquiescence of lazy or timid associates, by a crafty chief judge, who sophisticates the law to his mind, by the turn of his own reasoning" (Scalia 1994, 34). In fact, Jefferson wrote to Justice William Johnson in 1822, urging him to return to the English practice of individual opinions. "That of seriatim argument shows whether every judge has taken the trouble of understanding the case, of investigating it minutely, and of forming an opinion for himself, instead of pinning it on another's sleeve" (Scalia 1994, 34).

Finally, writing a concurrence can be personally satisfying to the justice.

> To be able to write an opinion solely for oneself, without the need to accommodate, to any degree whatever, the more-or-less differing views of one's colleagues; to address precisely the points of law

that one considers important and *no others*; to express precisely the degree of quibble, or foreboding, or disbelief, or indignation that one believes the majority's disposition should engender—that is indeed an unparalleled pleasure. (Scalia 1994, 42)

Thus, concurrences may be more revealing than justices' majority opinions because they are not the product of compromise (see Wahlbeck, et al. 1999). For example, Justice Frankfurter remarked that "[w]hen you have to have at least five people to agree on something, they can't have that comprehensive completeness of candor which is open to a single man, giving his own reasons untrammeled by what anybody else may do or not do if he put that out" (Phillips 1960, 298). Such analysis, moreover, might assist in discovering meaningful distinctions between justices of similar ideological beliefs. Additionally, because a concurrence indicates how a particular justice views a given issue, it may provide insight into how that justice may be expected to vote in the future. Given the significant legal and institutional consequences associated with concurring opinions, it is important for scholars to understand why a justice writes or joins a concurring opinion rather than silently joining the majority opinion. Moreover, it is important to understand what effect, if any, concurring opinions have on the lower courts and the Supreme Court.

Separate Opinion Writing and the Supreme Court

The Supreme Court is a powerful institution, co-equal with the other branches of government and prestigious enough that even though it is possessed of neither "purse, nor sword," the public accepts its rulings on matters ranging from abortion to sexual orientation, to even settling the dispute of who won the presidency. Although the Court makes decisions "within a legal framework" (Baum 2007, 2) there is no doubt that it is a political institution. The decisions handed down by the Supreme Court affect us in our everyday lives. Thus, it is important to understand how the justices reach these decisions. However, the justices operate in relative secrecy, discussing cases in private, without television cameras and reporters. Although recently this shroud of mystery has been penetrated (see, e.g., Lazarus 1998; Schwartz 1996; Woodward and Armstrong 1979), the predominant way the public has to understand the process by which the Supreme Court reaches its decisions is through its written opinions. Unlike Congress and the president, the Court must explain and justify its decisions and its policies in writing. The majority opinion of the Court is precedent that is binding on the lower courts. It becomes the law of the land, having an impact far beyond the parties in the litigation.

One reason for the power and prestige of the Court is the unanimity it exhibited in so many of its pivotal early rulings. Prior to the appointment of Chief Justice John Marshall, each justice delivered an opinion in each case, known as *seriatim* opinions. Marshall ended this practice because he believed that one opinion representing the decision of the Court would increase the Court's prestige and legitimacy. In fact, Marshall placed such a high value on a united front that not only did he go along with opinions that were contrary to his own view, he even announced some. Chief Justice Roberts decided to use Marshall as a model during his first term on the Supreme Court (Rosen 2006). Roberts believes that the unanimity achieved by Marshall is important to the legitimacy and credibility of the Court.[7] According to Roberts:

> There weren't a lot of concurring opinions in the thirty years when Marshall was the chief justice. There weren't a lot of dissents. And nowadays, you take a look at some of our opinions and you wonder if we're reverting back to the English model where everybody has to have their say. It's more being concerned with the jurisprudence of the individual rather than working toward a jurisprudence of the Court. (Rosen 2006, 224)

Are we back to *seriatim* opinions, as Roberts suggests? In the past fifty years, the number of separate opinions (concurrences and dissents) has increased dramatically. The predominant explanation for this increase has been framed in terms of institutional norms (see, e.g., Caldeira and Zorn 1998; Haynie 1992; O'Brien 1999; Walker, Epstein, and Dixon 1988). For example, Walker et al. attribute the increase in concurrences and dissents to the failed leadership of Chief Justice Stone.

Attitudinalists explain concurrences primarily as a function of policy preferences (see, e.g., Segal and Spaeth 2002).

> Those who join the majority opinion are ideologically closer to the opinion writer than those who write regular concurrences; regular concurrers, in turn, are ideologically closer to the majority opinion writer than special concurrers; and to complete the picture, special concurrers are ideologically closer to the majority opinion writer than are justices who dissent. (Segal and Spaeth 2002, 386–87)

On the other hand, proponents of the strategic model understand concurring opinions as part of the majority opinion coalition process. For example, Maltzman, et al. (2000) found that justices are less likely to write or join a concurrence if the author has cooperated with them in the past.

Although this line of scholarship has greatly enhanced our understanding of concurrences, it has either merged concurrences with dissents or has lumped concurrences together, basically treating them the same. I argue that the factors that influence a justice's decision to write or join a concurrence are different depending on the type of concurrence (the type of signal) being written.

Additionally, studies to date have ignored the effect of the rise of dissensus. Is the practice of separate opinion writing leading to a loss of confidence in the Court and in turn a lack of compliance by lower courts? Scholars argue that a decision that is accompanied by a concurrence speaks with less authority and can undermine the policy voice of the majority (Maveety 2005; Ray 1990). Moreover, concurring opinions are inconsistent with traditional consensus norms (Walker et al., 1988) and they represent "modes of conflict on the Supreme Court" (Caldeira and Zorn 1998, 877). Specifically, the argument is that the majority opinion is weakened by the presence of concurring opinions (see, e.g., Hansford and Spriggs 2006; Spriggs and Hansford 2001) and, consequently, the Supreme Court and the lower courts will be more likely to treat a precedent accompanied by a concurrence negatively. However, no one has examined the content of concurrences in an effort to explain whether the *type* of concurrence influences lower court compliance. The assumption in the previous literature is that all concurrences disagree with the majority opinion, and in fact, are similar to dissents. However, some concurrences support the majority opinion and others do not. For example, a concurring opinion may clarify the outcome of the case and strengthen the result. However, a concurrence can also detract from the impact of the majority opinion by disagreeing with the reasoning of the majority and pointing out the flaws of the opinion. Thus, differentiating between the types of concurrences can illuminate the true impact they have on treatment by subsequent courts.

Types of Concurrences

In order to systematically study Supreme Court opinions, datasets for the U.S. Supreme Court categorize or "code" opinions. This allows researchers to quantitatively assess decision making. To date, opinions are simply coded as either liberal or conservative. However,

> [a] decision to support Bakke's admission to the Davis's medical school represents a range of possible outcomes, from prohibiting race from being used as a factor (the Stevens position) to ruling that the state has a compelling interest in using race but the Davis

program is not narrowly drawn to meet that interest. Alternatively, ruling for Davis also represents a range of possible outcomes, not a single point on a scale. Since the decision on the merits only decides whether Bakke gets admitted, ruling for him means that Davis's program is to the right of a justice's indifference point, while ruling against him means that California's program is to the left of a justice's indifference point. (Segal and Spaeth 2003, 35)

Thus, Segal and Spaeth recognize that "by not coding concurrences in comparison to majority opinions, [they] do lose some information" (35). By understanding the content of the concurrences that are written or joined by the justices and understanding where they part company with the majority opinion, we gain a deeper understanding into the factors that influence justices' decision making and opinion writing and how the justices use concurrences to signal other actors. Two previous studies provide insight into how the justices use concurrences to signal other actors. I briefly discuss each of these works below and how they inform the typology I use in the present study.

In the *Manual on Appellate Court Opinions*, Witkin identifies the following different types of concurring opinions with illustrations: "Attempt to Expand Holding or To Supplement Reasoning," "Offering Different Theory to Support Conclusion," "Attempt to Limit or Qualify Holding," "Concurrence in Judgment Without Opinion," "Reluctant Concurrence," and the "Unnecessary Concurring Opinion." He also provides advice regarding their use, such as cautioning a judge against writing the concurrence in judgment without opinion. "This uninformative statement should be used sparingly. If the disagreement is not substantial, the main opinion ought to be signed; if the disagreement is substantial, the reason should be stated" (Witkin 1977, 223). Moreover, he argues that:

> [the] concurrence in its broadest sense is based on the right to participate in the formulation of the decision and opinion; and the collegial process is designed to explore and reconcile differences until a joint statement of the conclusion is drafted. Concurrences based on different grounds, or adding something that the majority refuses to accept, are justifiable; but a separate concurring opinion covering the same ground in a different way seems justifiable only after a genuine effort has been made to have the substance of the material incorporated into the main opinion. (Witkin 1977, 225)

Ray (1990) identifies the following concurrences: limiting, expansive, emphatic, and doctrinal. She then presents a qualitative analysis of the uses to which members of the Rehnquist Court have put the concurrence and then considers the effect of the concurrences on the Court's decision making process. She concludes that the concurrence can serve as an "instrument of judicial discourse," allowing "at once the principled expression of divergent views and the occupation of common ground" (Ray 1990, 831).

Thus, in the present study I code concurrences into the following categories: expansive; doctrinal; limiting; reluctant; emphatic; and unnecessary.[8] This typology is based on the categories described by Witkin (1977) and Ray (1990). I discuss each category below and provide examples of how each type is used in Supreme Court decision making.

The first category, the *expansive concurrence*, attempts to expand the holding or to supplement the reasoning of the majority opinion. It is "used to enlarge a holding by suggesting its application beyond the bounds of the majority opinion" (Ray 1990, 781). For example, in *Young v. U.S.* (1987) the Court held that an attorney for a party that is the beneficiary of a court order might not be appointed as a prosecutor in a contempt action that alleges the order was violated. Justice Blackmun concurred, stating: "I join Justice Brennan's opinion. I would go farther, however, and hold that the practice—federal or state—of appointing an interested party's counsel to prosecute for criminal contempt is a violation of due process" (*Young v. U.S.*, 1987, 814–15).

The second category is the *doctrinal concurrence*, which is a concurrence that offers a different theory to support the Court's result. This is the "right result, wrong reason" concurrence (Ray 1990, 800). This concurrence generally rejects the entire foundation of the Court's opinion, concurring in the judgment but for an entirely different reason. Thus, these concurrences disagree with the majority opinion, even though the opinion writer agrees with the final outcome of the case (who wins and who loses). For example, in *Connecticut v. Barrett* (1987) Justice Brennan wrote: "I concur in the judgment that the Constitution does not require the suppression of Barrett's statements to the police, *but for reasons different from those set forth in the opinion of the Court*" (530, italics added).

The third category is the *limiting concurrence*, a concurring opinion that attempts to limit or qualify the holding. The opinion writer argues that certain parts of the majority's discussion were unnecessary or thinks the Court has gone too far in its reasoning or conclusions. The "concurrer acts to rein in the doctrinal force of the majority" (Ray 1990, 784). The concurrence may limit the majority opinion to the particular circumstances of the case under review or may "take the majority to task for addressing an issue not properly before it" (Ray 1990, 785).

For example, in *Colorado v. Connelly* (1987), Justice Blackmun wrote:

> I join Parts I, II, III-B, and IV of the Court's opinion and its judgment. I refrain, however, from joining Part III-A of the opinion. Whatever may be the merits of the issue discussed there . . . that issue was neither raised nor briefed by the parties, and, in my view, it is not necessary to the decision. (171)

Another example is found in *Clarke v. Securities Industry Ass'n* (1987). In that case, Justice Stevens, joined by Chief Justice Rehnquist and Justice O'Connor, wrote:

> Analysis of the purposes of the branching limitations on national banks demonstrates that respondent is well within the "zone of interest" as that test has been applied in our prior decisions. Because I believe that these cases call for no more than a straightforward application of those prior precedents, I do not join Part II of the Court's opinion, which, in my view engages in a wholly unnecessary exegesis on the "zone of interest" test. (409–10)

The tendency for these limiting concurrences is toward contraction. Moreover, a limiting concurrence can signal to the lower court that support for the majority decision is not high, and provide a rationale for the lower court to not comply with the case.

The fourth category is the *reluctant concurrence*. Here, the opinion writer makes it clear that he does not want to join the majority's decision, but feels compelled to, perhaps because of precedent or because of a desire to produce a majority opinion on an important issue. An example is found in *Pope v. Illinois* (1987). In *Pope*, petitioners were convicted of obscenity under Illinois law when they sold certain magazines to police. They appealed based on the jury instruction given, which was that the jury must determine that the magazines were without "value" to convict and in order to make that determination, they must judge how the magazines would be viewed by ordinary citizens in the State of Illinois. The Court held that the proper inquiry was not whether an ordinary member of any given community would find value in the allegedly obscene material, but whether a reasonable person would find such value in the material.[9] Justice Scalia concurred with the opinion, writing:

> I join the Court's opinion with regard to an "objective" or "reasonable person" test of "serious literary, artistic, political, or scientific value," [citations omitted] because I think that the most faithful assessment of what *Miller* intended, and because we have not

been asked to reconsider *Miller* in the present case. I must note, however, that in my view it is quite impossible to come to an objective assessment of (at least) literary or artistic value, there being many accomplished people who have found literature in Dada, and art in the replication of a soup can. (504–05)

Scalia concluded his concurrence by stating that "[a]ll of today's opinions, I suggest, display the need for reexamination of *Miller*" (505).

Another example is Justice Brennan's concurrence in *Mathews v. United States* (1988). In *Mathews*, the petitioner was convicted for accepting a bribe. The trial court refused to instruct the jury as to entrapment because the petitioner did not admit all of the elements of the crime. In the majority opinion, the Court discussed the elements for a valid entrapment defense, which are government inducement of the crime and lack of a predisposition on the part of the defendant to engage in the criminal conduct. Predisposition focuses on whether the defendant was an "unwary innocent" or an "unwary criminal." Although he joined the majority opinion, which held that a defendant is not precluded from an entrapment instruction even if he denies one or more elements of the crime, Justice Brennan had dissented four times in cases holding, as *Mathews* did, "that the defendant's predisposition to commit a crime is relevant to the defense of entrapment" (66). Although it was clear from his concurrence that his views had not changed, he acknowledged that "I am not writing on a clean slate; the Court has spoken definitely on this point" (67). Thus, he "bow[ed] to stare decisis" (67).

The fifth category is the *emphatic concurrence*, which emphasizes some aspect of the Court's holding (see Ray 1990), and functions largely as a means of clarification. For example, in *INS v. Cardoza-Fonseca* (1987), INS began proceedings to deport Cardoza-Fonseca, and she applied for two forms of relief in the deportation hearings—asylum and withholding of deportation. An immigration judge denied her requests, finding that Cardoza-Fonseca had not established a "clear probability of persecution," which the judge believed was the standard for both claims. The Supreme Court held that a person is entitled to the discretionary relief of asylum if he shows he cannot return home because of "persecution or a well-founded fear of persecution" and a person is entitled to the mandatory relief of withholding deportation if he demonstrates a "clear probability of persecution" if he returns home. Blackmun's concurrence in *INS v. Cardoza-Fonseca* (1987) emphasized his understanding that the majority opinion directed the INS to appropriate sources to help it define the meaning of the "well-founded" fear standard and that the meaning would be refined in later litigation. Thus, the justice who writes or joins an emphatic concurrence is clarifying his or her understanding of the opinion.

Another example is provided by Justice Powell's concurrence in *F.C.C. v. Florida Power Corp.* (1987, 245). In this case, three cable operators alleged that the rates charged by utility companies for using utility poles for stringing television cable were unreasonable. The FCC set new rates under the Pole Attachments Act and the utility company filed suit, claiming the Act violated the Fifth Amendment's takings clause. The Supreme Court held that the Act did not constitute a "taking." Justice Powell concurred, "writ[ing] only to state generally my understanding as to the scope of judicial review of rates determined by an administrative agency."

Finally, the last category is the *unnecessary concurrence*, which is a concurrence in judgment without opinion. According to Witkin (1977), this type of concurrence "produces all the evils of a concurring opinion with none of its values; i.e., it casts doubt on the principles declared in the main opinion without indicating why they are wrong or questionable" (223). This type of concurrence could mean that the concurring justice does not agree with the principles in the majority opinion, or that he agrees with them but not with the reasoning or authorities set forth to support them, or that he agrees with only some of the principles, or that he neither agrees nor disagrees, or that he objects to something in the opinion (perhaps a quote, humor or satire, or even punishment of a litigant) and withholds his signature because the majority opinion writer would not take it out. However, because the justice has not revealed why he or she is concurring, one is left to speculate regarding the possible reason.

Outline of the Book

In order to understand concurring opinion writing on the U.S. Supreme Court, in Chapter 2 I use the typology mentioned earlier to explain why a justice writes or joins a concurring opinion rather than silently joining the majority. This typology is important because it shows the way the justices engage in a dialogue about the law and communicate their relationship to the majority opinion and their preferences about legal rules. By categorizing concurrences into different types and distinguishing between concurrences, I show that some concurrences support the majority decision, whereas others do not. Some concurrences contract the majority decision, whereas others expand the reach of the majority decision. My theory is that different types of concurrences are influenced by different factors, which I show by using a multinomial logit model.

In Chapter 3, I provide a qualitative analysis of the bargaining and accommodation that occurs on the Supreme Court in order to understand why concurrences are published. When are efforts at bargaining successful and when do they fail? Do concurring opinions result from failed negotiations? Using the private papers of Justices Harry A. Blackmun and Thurgood Marshall, I show that, although policy objectives clearly affect the justices' behavior, there are other factors that come into play.

In Chapter 4, I assess the impact that concurring opinions have on lower court compliance. Additionally, I examine the impact that concurring opinions have on the Supreme Court's interpretation of its own precedent. I show that concurrences do matter, but that it is important to understand what type of concurrence accompanies a majority opinion.

Using the foregoing methodologies, I show the value of exploring the content of concurrences. Treating concurrences as disagreement or lumping concurrences together without differentiating between them camouflages the true influence of attitudinal and nonattitudinal factors. The factors that influence a justice's decision whether to write or join a concurrence are different depending on what type of concurrence is being written. Specifically, the decision to write or join a particular type of concurrence is a complex decision that involves justice-specific, case-specific, and institutional factors. By examining the memoranda between Blackmun and Marshall and the other justices and the memoranda from their clerks, additional insight is gained into the bargaining and accommodation that occurs on the Supreme Court, with an emphasis on how concurring opinions are created. Finally, the justices of the Supreme Court, by using concurrences as judicial signals, have the potential to influence the impact that the majority decision has on lower courts and on how the Supreme Court treats its own precedent in the future. This book shows the importance of differentiating between the impact a justice has by joining the majority on the merits vote and the impact the justice has in the actual language used in the concurrence he or she writes or joins. All of this demonstrates the importance and necessity of taking a first step toward that final goal: explaining the actual content of Court opinions.

2

Why Justices Write or Join

Modeling Concurring Behavior

In *Washington v. Glucksberg* (1997) the Court addressed whether the Constitution provides any right to a physician's assistance in ending one's life. Specifically, *Glucksberg* involved Washington's ban on "promoting a suicide attempt" (705). The state defined this crime as "knowingly caus[ing] or aid[ing] another person to attempt suicide" (705). Chief Justice Rehnquist wrote the Court's opinion, which was joined by O'Connor, Scalia, Kennedy, and Thomas. Rehnquist phrased the issue at a very high level of generality: "whether the 'liberty' specially protected by the Due Process Clause includes a right to commit suicide which itself includes a right to assistance in doing so" (723). The Court concluded that there was no fundamental right to commit suicide and that the state's interest in regulating suicide was rational. Thus, the statute was upheld.

O'Connor supplied the critical fifth vote in support of Rehnquist's opinion, and wrote a concurrence. Rehnquist's opinion essentially sought to close the door on any arguments concerning a fundamental right associated with assisted suicide. O'Connor, although agreeing that the Constitution does not protect a "generalized right to 'commit suicide,'" (797) mentioned a narrower issue about which she reserved judgment, namely "whether a mentally competent person who is experiencing great suffering has a constitutionally cognizable interest in controlling the circumstances of his or her imminent death" (798).

Why did O'Connor choose to write this concurrence? What determines the type of concurring opinion a justice chooses to write or join? I argue that different types of concurrences are influenced by different factors. Here, I focus on cases decided during the 1986–1989 terms. Using the Justice-Centered Rehnquist Court Database (Benesh and Spaeth 2003), I code each concurrence accompanying the majority opinion according to the typology described in Chapter 1. A list of each case, along with the code assigned to each concurrence and the justice who wrote the concurrence, is contained in the appendix.

Rise in Concurring Opinions

Chief Justice Marshall was responsible for the tradition of consensus on the Supreme Court. Marshall changed the practice of each justice writing an opinion in each case—*seriatim* opinions—to one opinion representing the decision of the Court. In fact, Marshall discouraged separate opinions, believing that unanimous decisions would increase the Court's prestige and legitimacy. Justice Samuel Chase wrote the first concurrence during the Marshall Court, issuing a one-sentence concurrence in an 1804 insurance case.[1] Justice Bushrod Washington followed the next year with the Marshall Court's first recorded dissent.[2]

With the rise of individual opinions, the majority opinion has become devalued (see O'Brien 1999). "[W]hen individual opinions are more highly prized than opinions for the Court, consensus not only declines but the Court's rulings appear more fragmented, uncertain, less stable, and less predictable" (O'Brien 1999, 111). Figure 2.1 shows the rise of separate opinion writing on the Supreme Court.[3]

The predominant explanation for separate opinion writing has been framed in terms of institutional norms. Walker, et al. (1988) described the

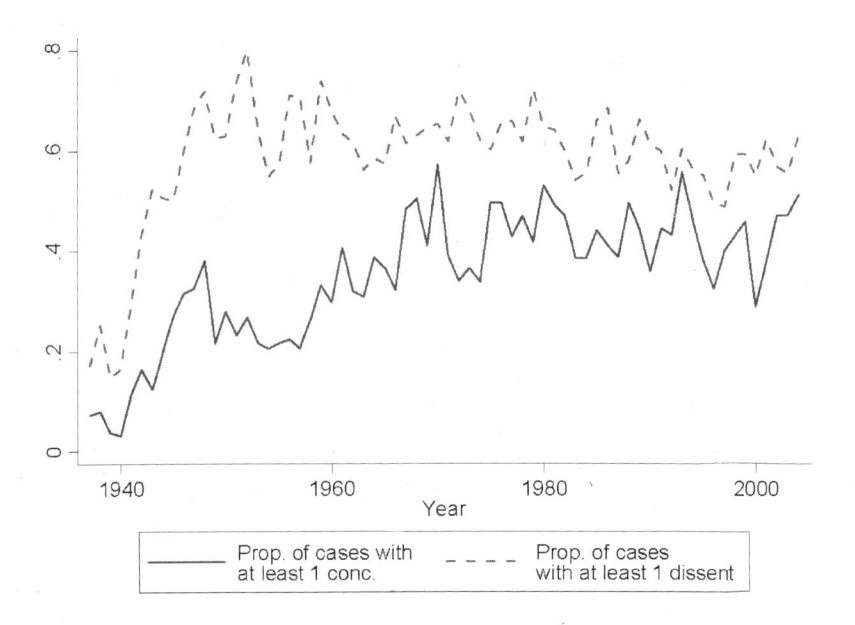

Figure 2.1. Proportion of Cases with Concurring and Dissenting Opinions, 1937–2004 Terms.

increase in dissenting and concurring opinions as changing norms of the Supreme Court, altering "the Court's decision-making regime" (362). They examined the following factors possibly contributing to the increasing rates of concurring and dissenting opinions: (a) Congressional enactment of the Judiciary Act of 1925; (b) changes in the Court's caseload; (c) the promotion of a sitting associate to be chief justice; (d) changes in the Court's composition; and (e) the leadership of the chief justice. They concluded, "much of the responsibility for changing the operational norms of the Court from institutional unity to permitting free expression of individual views can be attributed to the leadership of Harlan Fiske Stone" (Walker, et al. 1988, 384).

Haynie (1992), building on the work of Walker, et al. (1988), investigated the effects of individual leadership styles using a time-series analysis. Haynie's research distinguished between concurring and dissenting opinions, finding that the increase in concurring opinions occurred not during Stone's tenure but during that of Chief Justice Hughes and continued under Chief Justice Stone. "[T]he additional analysis of the rise of concurring opinions helps to unravel the puzzle. It appears that under Hughes, cohorts were indeed more likely to express their disagreement with the means to the ends. They were not as willing to express their disagreement with the means *and* the ends" (Haynie 1992, 1167).

O'Brien (1999) argues that the increase in dissenting and concurring opinions preceded Stone's chief justiceship. He attributes the demise of the norm of consensus to the legal liberalism brought by the New Deal justices. "They quickly began disagreeing and pursuing their differences over conflicting tenets of liberal legalism in individual opinions" (O'Brien 1999, 103).

Caldeira and Zorn (1998) researched the levels of concurrence and dissent on the Court, arguing that they are functions of "consensual norms," norms that are influenced by the behaviors of the individual justices. These norms cause concurrences and dissents to fluctuate around a common level. They found that dissents and concurrences move together over time, evidence that consensual norms appear to influence substantially both concurrences and dissents on the Court.

Although all of these studies have greatly increased our understanding of the influences on concurrences in the aggregate, we still do not understand why an individual justice chooses to write or join a concurrence. What influences the type of signal the justice is sending? The next section addresses the studies that have examined concurrences on an individual level.

Explaining Concurrences on an Individual Level

The dominant model of Supreme Court decision making is the attitudinal model (Segal and Spaeth 2002). Proponents of this model view the justices of the Supreme Court as policy-oriented actors who vote their true policy preferences. "Simply put, Rehnquist vote[d] the way he [did] because he [was] extremely conservative; Marshall voted the way he did because he was extremely liberal" (Segal and Spaeth 2002, 86).

Attitudinalists explain concurrences primarily as a function of their policy preferences.

> Those who join the majority opinion are ideologically closer to the opinion writer than those who write regular concurrences; regular concurrers, in turn, are ideologically closer to the majority opinion writer than special concurrers; and to complete the picture, special concurrers are ideologically closer to the majority opinion writer than are justices who dissent. (Segal and Spaeth 2002, 386–87)

Segal and Spaeth (2002) addressed special concurrences in an attempt to understand why a justice writes a special concurrence. Specifically, they analyzed the "culpability" index for each justice, which they explain is the extent to which each justice allows his or her policy preferences to prevent the Court from forming a majority opinion coalition in a given case. Specifically, the "culpability" index is based on the number of special concurrences that prevented a majority opinion coalition from forming. They did not find much differentiation among the justices, concluding that attitudes were not responsible for the justices' behavior. Instead, they reasoned that individual personality characteristics were responsible for a justice choosing to write or join a special concurrence. This examination, in addition to focusing only on special concurrences, did not address any other variables that would explain concurring opinion writing.

Rational-choice explanations predicting that justices act strategically begin with the underlying premise of the attitudinal model, but proponents of this model argue that there are constraints placed on the justices that make it impossible for them to achieve their true preferences (see Epstein and Knight 1998; Maltzman, et al. 2000). Thus, justices may take positions that do not represent their true ideal point in order to maximize their preferences when they know they cannot win on their true preferences.

Strategic approaches to judicial decision making understand concurring opinions as part of the majority opinion coalition process (see, e.g., Maltzman, et al. 2000). One recent study examined why an individual chooses to author or join a separate opinion (Wahlbeck, et al. 1999). Using data from the Burger Court, the authors tested the influence of attitudinal, strategic, and institutional factors on justices' decisions to author or join a regular concurrence, special concurrence, or a dissent, as opposed to joining the majority opinion. They found that the willingness of a justice to disagree with the majority's legal reasoning stems from a combination of attitudinal, strategic, and institutional factors. Specifically with respect to concurrences, they found that the farther a justice is ideologically from the majority opinion author, the more likely he or she is to write or join a special concurrence or a regular concurrence. Although the complexity of a case increases a justice's tendency to write a concurrence, it has no effect on the decision to join a concurrence. They also found that justices are less likely to write or join a concurrence if the majority opinion author has cooperated with them in the past. Political and legal salience also generally increase the chances that a justice will concur. Furthermore, in a case involving a minimum winning conference coalition, justices are less likely to write or join a special concurrence. With regard to institutional factors, they found that Chief Justice Burger was less likely to write special concurrences and that justices are less likely to write a concurrence as the end of the Court's term approaches. However, this study, with the exception of differentiating between regular and special concurrences, treated all concurrences exactly the same. Thus, although we are beginning to understand the factors that influence an individual justice's decision to write or join a concurrence rather than silently joining the majority opinion, we still do not understand why a justice decides to write or join a *particular type* of concurring opinion.

Scholars recently have turned their attention to concurrences in an effort to understand opinion writing (see Maveety 2002, 2003; Turner and Way 2003; Way and Turner 2006). Maveety (2002) argues that concurrences show that judicial policy goals should be thought of as bifurcated: policy in case outcomes, and policy in doctrinal rules. This means that justices achieve their policy goals when they vote for the outcome and they achieve their doctrinal goals through concurrences. In one study, Maveety (2003) presented a preliminary research design, using data from the 2002 term. She examined the doctrinal messages of the concurring opinions in that term in order to show substantive disagreement between the concurring opinion and the opinion of the Court over the policy and she examined the content of "choral" concurring opinions in order to show communication of legal debate among the justices in majority coalitions. Way and Turner (2006) also analyzed the content of concurrences by coding them according to four broad themes: ground laying, signaling, preserving, and weakening. They coded the concurrences written by the Rehnquist Court justices between the 1991 and 2001 terms. They found that several institutional factors, including citations to previous cases, the number of justices joining the concurrence, and the extent to which the author joins the majority opinion are important predictors of the type of concurrence. However, this study did not address many relevant variables, such as importance of the case. Additionally, although the study did address ideology, it did not address any other justice-specific factors. In the next section, I develop an explanatory model to account for why a justice joins or writes a particular type of concurrence rather than silently joining the majority decision.

Specifying a Model of Concurring Opinion Writing

For the most part, previous literature has either merged concurrences with dissents or has treated all different types of concurrences as the same, with the exception of differentiating between regular and special concurrences. Additionally, the concurring opinion is characterized as dissensus, described as "leav[ing] an impression of dissonance within the tribunal" (Schwartz 1957, 351). However, as explained in Chapter 1, some concurrences support the majority opinion, whereas others do not. Specifically, limiting, doctrinal, and reluctant concurrences are not completely supportive of the majority decision, whereas expansive and emphatic concurrences are. Although unnecessary concurrences do not support the reasoning of the decision, they do not provide any reasons for the refusal to sign on to the majority opinion. The model I constructed here takes into account these differences in concurrences.

Justice-Specific Factors

Ideology plays a part in determining the type of concurring opinion. One would expect that a limiting concurrence is more likely to be written by a liberal justice who signs on to a conservative decision or by a conservative justice signing on to a liberal opinion. A limiting concurrence may signal to a lower court a strategy for limiting the scope of the majority's reasoning. Similarly, an expansive concurrence is more likely to be written by the most liberal justice who signs on to a liberal decision or by the most conservative justice voting for a conservative decision.

Ideology also should influence the decision to author a reluctant concurrence because the author does not want to join the majority opinion, yet feels compelled to because of institutional reasons, such as precedent or the desire to produce a badly needed majority opinion.

In order to evaluate these hypotheses empirically, I use a measure of individual justice ideology interacted with the ideological direction of the case. The measure is the difference between the majority opinion writer and the justice's Segal–Cover scores (Segal and Cover 1989).[4] I then interacted that difference with directional dummies for the decisions (1 = conservative decision, −1 = liberal decision). Thus, the variable is negative if the justice is either less liberal than the majority opinion writer in a liberal decision or less conservative than the majority opinion writer in a conservative decision and the variable is positive if the justice is more liberal than the majority opinion writer in a liberal decision and more conservative than the majority opinion writer in a conservative decision.

Scholars have found that justices with certain personal background characteristics, such as being a former law school professor, write concurrences in a larger proportion of cases (see Brenner and Heberlig 2002). This may be because justices accept the professional norms and incentives of academics to express and publish their own views. In short, academia encourages the expression of disagreement. Do these justice-specific characteristics influence the *type* of concurrence a justice writes or joins? I would expect justices who previously taught at a law school to be more sensitive to the nuances of the law and its language; thus, it follows that these justices would be more likely to write or join limiting, expansive, or doctrinal concurrences because these types of concurrences are either concerned with the policy implications of the majority opinion or are an effort to shape the direction of the law. The measure for having previously taught at a law school is dichotomous (1 = did; 0 = did not). Data on each justice were obtained from the U.S. Supreme Court Compendium (Epstein, Segal, Spaeth, and Walker 2007).

Finally, cooperation has been shown to influence separate opinion writing on the Supreme Court (see Wahlbeck, et al. 1999; Maltzman, et al., 2000). In short, justices use a tit-for-tat strategy during the opinion writing process.

> Strategic justices recognize another form of interdependency of choice—the nature of the cooperative relationship between pairs of justices. Because justices are engaged in long-term relationships with their colleagues, over time justices presumably learn to cooperate and engage in reciprocity, rewarding those who have cooperated with them in the past and punishing others. (Maltzman, et al. 2000, 20–21)

For example, Segal and Spaeth (1993) suggest that justices are more likely to write separately when O'Connor is the majority opinion writer because of her tendency to write separate opinions. Thus, I posit that past interactions between the justices should affect their decisions regarding what type of concurrence to write. Since limiting and doctrinal opinions arguably detract from the message of the majority, I expect that these types of opinions will be less likely if the justice has a cooperative relationship with the majority opinion writer. To measure cooperation between the justices, I use Westerland's (2004) measure of cooperation, which is the agreement rate for nonmajority opinions (regular concurrences, special concurrences, and dissents), which is then multiplied for each justice dyad in each term. For example, Scalia joined 33 percent of Thomas's nonmajority opinions in 2000, whereas Thomas joined 41 percent of Scalia's nonmajority opinions for that term. Thus, their cooperation score for that term is .14, which is .33 multiplied by .41.[5]

Case-Specific Factors

Scholars have argued that when a case is more complex, it is less likely that the opinion will reflect a justice's policy preferences, which will lead to more separate opinions (see Wahlbeck, et al. 1999). Because limiting and doctrinal opinions do not wholeheartedly support the policy articulated by the majority, I expect that when a case is complex, a justice will be more likely to join or author either a limiting or doctrinal concurrence. Moreover, an emphatic concurrence may be prompted by its author's inability to negotiate the insertion of some clarifying language into an otherwise acceptable majority opinion (see Ray 1990). Thus, an emphatic concurrence may be more likely to be joined or written in complex cases, where it is more difficult to accommodate all of the justices. I count the number of legal provisions relied on and the number of legal issues raised in the precedent (see Benesh and Reddick 2002) as a way to measure complex cases.

Another relevant consideration for the justices is the importance of the case to them and also to external political actors and the public. In unimportant cases, justices may be willing to ignore their preferences and create an illusion of consensus. Furthermore, the policy implications of an important case are broader. Thus, I expect that a justice will be more likely to write or join a limiting or expansive concurrence if the case is important. Additionally, I expect that a justice will be more likely to write or join a doctrinal concurrence in an important case because the justice wishes to alter and shape the direction of the law in the future. Finally, the emphatic concurrence may be more likely to be written or joined in important cases in order to provide clarity.

I include two variables to assess importance. The first is a measure of political salience, coded 1 if the case is a major case using *The New York Times* measure, and 0 otherwise (Epstein and Segal 2000).[6] The second is a measure of legal salience, which is measured as whether an opinion overturned precedent or declared a state or federal law unconstitutional. This was determined by using the Justice-Centered Rehnquist Court Database (Benesh and Spaeth 2003). If a case overruled one or more of the Court's own precedents or overturned a piece of state or federal legislation, I coded the case as 1, 0 otherwise.

Previous research has shown that when a winning coalition is small, majority opinion authors seek to accommodate their colleagues (see Murphy 1964; Wahlbeck, Spriggs and Maltzman 1998). Wahlbeck, et al. (1999) found that justices in a minimum winning, majority conference coalition are less likely to write or join a special concurrence. Because doctrinal concurrences disagree with the reasoning of the Court, and, consequently, are more likely to be classified as special concurrences, a doctrinal concurrence probably is less likely to be written or joined in cases involving a minimum winning coalition.[7] Additionally, it is probably the case that a limiting concurrence is less likely in cases involving a minimum winning coalition. The reason for this expectation is because in the case of *Marks v. United States* (1977), the Supreme Court formalized the "narrowest grounds doctrine." According to this doctrine, when a fragmented Court decides a case and no single rationale explaining the result has the vote of five justices, "the holding of the Court may be viewed as that position taken by those Members who concurred in the judgments on the narrowest grounds" (193). Thus, in cases involving a minimum winning coalition, the majority opinion writer should be more likely to accommodate the justice who wishes to limit the reach of the majority opinion because if he does not, that justice may be in a position to control the policy promulgated by the Court.

Additionally, the emphatic concurrence has been described as the safety valve that permits a justice to join with or make possible a majority (Ray 1990). By allowing its author to clarify his or her understanding of the Court's holding, the emphatic concurrence may in some instances work to create a fragile consensus. If this is true, the emphatic concurrence may be used more often in closely divided cases, such as cases involving minimum winning coalitions.

The measure I use for minimum winning coalition is from the Justice-Centered Rehnquist Court Database (Benesh and Spaeth 2003) and is coded 1 if yes, 0 otherwise. If coded 1, this means the reported vote in the case was decided by a one-vote margin or by a two-vote margin when the winning coalition has five votes or less. Therefore, minimum winning coalitions are those decided by 5–4 and 4–3, or by a 5–3 or 4–2 vote that reverses the decision of the lower court.

Institutional Factors

The chief justice is in a special position given his institutional role, and, consequently, is less likely to write concurring and dissenting opinions (see Brenner and Heberlig 2002), perhaps because he is likely to believe that writing dissenting and concurring opinions will reflect a lack of leadership on the Court. O'Brien (1999) explained that Rehnquist wrote fewer dissenting and concurring opinions after becoming chief. Additionally, research has shown that chief justices are less likely to write or join special concurrences (Wahlbeck, et al. 1999). Thus, given that limiting, doctrinal, and reluctant concurring opinions do not support the majority opinion, I expect that Rehnquist is less likely to write or join those types of opinions. Furthermore, the unnecessary concurrence, although it does not provide a reason for the disagreement, does not join the majority opinion, merely concurring in the outcome. Therefore, Rehnquist is less likely to note an unnecessary concurrence.[8] I coded each observation for Chief Justice Rehnquist as 1, 0 otherwise.

Acclimation effects may influence the type of concurrence the justice chooses to write or join (see Hettinger, Lindquist and Martinek 2003; Wahlbeck, et al. 1999). New justices do not have any Supreme Court experience to guide their behavior. They must acclimate themselves to their new environment, learning the expectations of the Court, and the different norms and procedures (see Hettinger, et al. 2003; 2006). This means that new justices may be more likely to avoid conflict or vote more moderately because they are unsure about their place on the Court. Thus, I expect that "freshman" justices will be less likely to write or join the concurrences that are less supportive of the majority opinion: limiting, doctrinal, and reluctant. I created a freshmen variable, which was coded 1 if a justice had served less than two complete terms on the bench, 0 otherwise.

Table 2.1 summarizes the hypotheses presented here.

Table 2.1. Summary of Hypotheses

Variable	Type of Concurrence Influenced
Justice-specific	
Ideological compatibility	Limiting, expansive, reluctant
Taught law	Limiting, expansive, doctrinal
Cooperation	Limiting, doctrinal
Case-specific	
Complexity	Limiting, doctrinal, emphatic
Importance	Limiting, expansive, doctrinal, emphatic
Minimum winning coalition	Doctrinal, emphatic, limiting
Institutional	
Chief justice	Limiting, doctrinal, reluctant, unnecessary
Freshman justice	Limiting, doctrinal, reluctant

Estimating a Model of Concurring Opinion Writing

Having developed a comprehensive explanation of an individual justice's decision to write or join a particular type of concurrence rather than joining the majority, I now test this explanation using empirical data. As stated earlier, the data to test these hypotheses come from the Justice-Centered Rehnquist Court Database for the terms 1986 through 1989 (Benesh and Spaeth 2003). The population is all orally argued, signed opinions. Because this study focuses on justices who agree with the result, I excluded the observations in which the justice dissented. I also excluded opinions concurring in part and dissenting in part, because they do not accept the Court's judgment in its entirety (Ray 1990).[9] Finally, I excluded the observations where the justice was the majority opinion writer, given that I am explaining why justices decide to write or join concurring opinions.[10]

Of the 3,033 justice observations, 2,646 (87%) joined the majority opinion, whereas 387 (13%) of the observations involved a justice writing or joining a concurrence. Of those 387 observations, 120 (31%) were limiting concurrences, 16 (4%) were reluctant, 53 (14%) expansive, 51 (13%) emphatic, 138 (36%) doctrinal, and 9 (2%) unnecessary. Although a majority of the concurrences are expressing disagreement in some fashion with the majority opinion, more than 25 percent of the concurrences are quite supportive of the majority decision. Thus, treating all concurrences as disagreement masks important differences and variations among the justices' behavior.

Table 2.2 (next page) presents the type of concurrence written or joined by each justice.

As shown in Table 2.2, limiting and doctrinal concurrences are used more frequently by a majority of the justices who choose to write or join a concurrence. Thus, it appears that the concurrence is mostly used as a way to contract and limit the reach of the majority opinion or used as a "right result, wrong reason" device. Chief Justice Rehnquist wrote or joined the limiting concurrence the most as a percentage of the total concurrences (35.7%) although he only wrote or joined fourteen concurring opinions. Scalia, on the other hand, wrote or joined seventy-six concurring opinions. Marshall and Brennan wrote or joined the doctrinal concurrence the most as a percentage of their total (53% and 45.2%, respectively). Clearly, concurrences serve as a way for the justices to express their preferences not just with the disposition of the case (who wins and who loses), but also over the substantive policy that the opinion represents.

The dependent variable is the type of concurrence. I estimated a multinomial logit model on a seven-category dependent variable: justice joins majority opinion, justice writes or joins a limiting, reluctant, expansive, emphatic, doctrinal, or an unnecessary concurrence. Multinomial logit is the appropriate

Table 2.2. Types of Concurrences, by Justice (1986–1989)

Type of Concurrence

Justice	Limiting	Reluctant	Expansive	Emphatic	Doctrinal	Unnecessary	Total (100%)
Marshall	10 (31.3%)	1 (3.1%)	2 (6.3%)	2 (6.3%)	17 (53%)	0 (0.0%)	32
Brennan	11 (26.2%)	2 (4.8%)	4 (9.5%)	6 (14.3%)	19 (45.2%)	0 (0.0%)	42
White	7 (20.0%)	5 (14.3%)	4 (11.4%)	9 (25.7%)	9 (25.7%)	1 (2.9%)	35
Blackmun	15 (28.8%)	2 (3.9%)	5 (9.6%)	8 (15.4%)	18 (34.6%)	4 (7.7%)	52
Powell*	3 (33.3%)	0 (0.0%)	1 (11.1%)	4 (44.4%)	1 (11.1%)	0 (0.0%)	9
Rehnquist	5 (35.7%)	1 (7.1%)	2 (14.3%)	4 (28.6%)	2 (14.3%)	0 (0.0%)	14
Stevens	17 (32.1%)	3 (5.7%)	10 (18.9%)	4 (7.5%)	19 (35.8%)	0 (0.0%)	53
O'Connor	15 (31.9%)	0 (0.0%)	7 (14.9%)	7 (14.9%)	16 (34.0%)	2 (4.3%)	47
Scalia	27 (35.5%)	1 (1.3%)	12 (15.8%)	4 (5.3%)	30 (39.5%)	2 (2.6%)	76
Kennedy	10 (37.0%)	1 (3.7%)	6 (22.2%)	3 (11.1%)	7 (26.0%)	0 (0.0%)	27
Total	120	16	53	51	138	9	387

*Due to rounding, the total percentage does not add up to 100.

estimator when the dependent variable is a nominal variable with multiple categories (Long and Freese 2001). Because this technique estimates the likelihood that an action will be chosen compared with another alternative, which serves as a base, it provides six sets of estimates. In this model, joining the majority opinion serves as the base. Table 2.3 summarizes the results, indicating which variables did, in fact, influence the type of concurrence written and the direction of the substantive effect. This table shows the likelihood that a judge will file a particular type of concurrence relative to the likelihood of simply joining the majority opinion. For interested readers, the full statistical results of the multinomial logit estimation appear in the appendix, along with descriptive statistics for all of the independent variables.

As Table 2.3 (next page) indicates, ideological compatibility between the justice and the majority opinion writer, interacted with the ideological direction of the majority decision, decreases the likelihood of a reluctant concurrence; however, this variable has no effect on writing or joining an expansive or limiting concurrence.

As expected, teaching law increases the likelihood of a limiting or an expansive concurrence. Justices who have taught at a law school are perhaps more sensitive to the language of the law. They have experience analyzing the language of opinions, and how lower courts and the Supreme Court interpret that language. Both limiting and expansive concurrences either are concerned with the policy implications of the majority opinion or are an effort to shape the direction of the law. Thus, these types of concurrences are more likely when the justice has previous experience as a law professor.

Cooperation decreases the likelihood of limiting or doctrinal concurrences, as expected, and also decreases the likelihood of an emphatic concurrence, which is surprising. Perhaps because an emphatic concurrence merely emphasizes some aspect of the Court's holding, the fact that a justice writes this type of concurrence reflects the inability of the justice and the majority opinion writer to bargain successfully over the language of the opinion. This seems more likely to be the case when the justices do not have a cooperative relationship.

The case-specific variables are good predictors of the likelihood of the types of concurrences written or joined by the justices. As the number of issues and legal provisions increases, limiting, emphatic, or doctrinal concurrences are more likely. Important cases, both politically important and legally important, are related to the types of concurrences. Additionally, if a case involves a minimum winning coalition, the majority opinion writer is more likely to bargain with the justice, leading to a decreased likelihood of limiting or doctrinal concurrences.

Variables relating to institutional roles help predict the occurrence of specific types of concurrences. The chief justice is less likely to write or join a

Table 2.3. Results of Concurrence Model

Variable	Limiting vs. Join Majority	Reluctant vs. Join Majority	Expansive vs. Join Majority	Emphatic vs. Join Majority	Doctrinal vs. Join Majority	Unnecessary vs. Join Majority
Justice-Specific						
Ideological compatibility	No effect	Less likely	No effect	No effect	No effect	No effect
Taught law	More likely	No effect	More likely	No effect	No effect	No effect
Cooperation	Less likely	No effect	No effect	Less likely	Less likely	Less likely
Case-Specific						
Complexity	More likely	No effect	No effect	More likely	More likely	No effect
Importance						
Political importance	No effect	No effect	More likely	More likely	No effect	No effect
Legal importance	More likely	No effect	More likely	No effect	No effect	No effect
Minimum winning coalition	Less likely	No effect	No effect	No effect	Less likely	Less likely
Institutional						
Chief justice	Less likely	No effect	No effect	No effect	Less likely	Less likely
Freshman justice	Less likely	No effect	No effect	No effect	No effect	No effect

limiting, doctrinal, or unnecessary concurrence because of collegiality concerns and a freshman justice is less likely to write or join a limiting concurrence.

Table 2.3 and the discussion so far have focused simply on which factors matter and whether they make a particular type of concurrence more or less likely. Table 2.4 (next page) provides the meaning of the statistical results in substantive terms. Based on the full estimation results (reported in the appendix), Table 2.4 presents a variety of predicted probabilities for each of the statistically significant variables. The first row of the table shows the baseline predicted probability of joining the majority opinion or writing a particular type of concurrence. These baseline probabilities are computed by holding all continuous variables (such as ideological compatibility and cooperation) at their mean values, while holding all discrete variables (such as legal salience and chief justice) at their modal values. The resulting probabilities are the equivalent of the average probability of observing each outcome and provide a useful starting point for evaluating the magnitude of the influence of each variable. As reported in Table 2.4, the likelihood of writing or joining any type of concurrence is quite low. Specifically, the probability of a doctrinal concurrence is the highest at .039. The probability of a limiting concurrence is .030, the probability of a reluctant concurrence is .005, the probability of an expansive concurrence is .011, and the probability of an emphatic concurrence is .018.

The remaining rows in Table 2.4 report the predicted probabilities for each outcome as I allow each statistically significant variable to take on different values, while holding all of the other variables constant at their respective baseline values.

Consider first the teaching law variable. As noted previously, this variable matters in terms of predicting limiting and expansive concurrences. Comparing the baseline predicted probabilities of observing a limiting and expansive concurrence (in which the justice has not taught law) with the predicted probabilities of observing a limiting and expansive concurrence when the justice has experience teaching law gives a sense of the substantive effects of this variable. The difference in absolute terms is rather small, with a .02 increase in the probability of a limiting concurrence and a .01 increase in the probability of an expansive concurrence. The fact that these changes are small in absolute terms is not at all surprising given that the likelihood of any type of concurrence is quite small to begin with. When the effects are considered in terms of percentage change, the effects are quite substantial, with the probability of a limiting concurrence almost twice as likely and an expansive concurrence about twice as likely if the justice has experience teaching law.

A legally important case has a great effect on the probability of a limiting and expansive concurrence. Both types of concurrences are twice as likely

Table 2.4. Predicted Probabilities of Justices' Decisions to Write or Join a Specific Type of Concurrence Versus Joining the Majority Opinion (1986–1989 Terms)

Variable	Probability of Limiting Concurrence	Probability of Reluctant Concurrence	Probability of Expansive Concurrence	Probability of Emphatic Concurrence	Probability of Doctrinal Concurrence	Probability of Unnecessary Concurrence
Baseline	.030	.005	.011	.018	.039	.001
Justice less liberal in liberal decision or less conservative in conservative decision	n.s.	.012	n.s.	n.s.	n.s.	n.s.
Justice more liberal in liberal decision or more conservative in conservative decision	n.s.	.002	n.s.	n.s.	n.s.	n.s.
Taught law	.051	n.s.	.021	n.s.	n.s.	n.s.
Minimum level of Cooperation (0)	.047	n.s.	n.s.	.026	.065	.003
Maximum level of Cooperation (.785714)	.000	n.s.	n.s.	.000	.000	.000
Minimum level of Complexity (2)	.028	n.s.	n.s.	.016	.037	n.s.
Maximum level of Complexity (9)	.102	n.s.	n.s.	.067	.092	n.s.

Politically important case	n.s.	n.s.	.019	.035	n.s.	n.s.
Legally important case	.060	n.s.	.022	n.s.	n.s.	n.s.
Minimum winning coalition case	.016	n.s.	n.s.	n.s.	.011	.000
Chief justice	.013	n.s.	n.s.	n.s.	.005	.000
Freshman justice	.020	n.s.	n.s.	n.s.	n.s.	n.s.

if the case overturned precedent or declared a state or federal law unconstitutional. Whether a case involves a minimum winning coalition strongly affects whether a justice writes or joins a doctrinal concurrence, decreasing the predicted probability by .028. Since a doctrinal concurrence disagrees with the reasoning employed by the majority and also is more likely to be a special concurrence, meaning the justice does not sign on to the majority opinion, the majority opinion writer has great incentive to bargain successfully with the justice in cases involving a minimum winning coalition in order to create binding precedent. The chief justice is also much less likely to write or join a doctrinal concurrence, decreasing the predicted probability from .039 to .005 and he is much less likely to write or join a limiting concurrence, with the predicted probability decreasing by more than 50 percent.

In the discussion of substantive results so far, I have discussed the effect of a single variable on the probability of the justice writing or joining a specific type of concurrence. Next, I set several variables to hypothetical values and I compute the predicted probability associated with the different combination of values. I find that, although the baseline probabilities are quite low, they can vary quite dramatically.

For example, take a case that is politically important, legally important, and complex. Additionally, the case does not involve a minimum winning coalition. The particular justice is not the chief justice and is not a freshman. The justice has experience teaching law and the justice does not have a cooperative relationship with the majority opinion writer. When I compute the probability of the likelihood of this hypothetical justice writing or joining a limiting concurrence based on these assumed values, I find that the predicted probability is .401. Thus, although the baseline probability of observing a limiting concurrence is quite low and the effect of any single variable is minimal, a combination of factors results in a much higher likelihood of that particular type of concurrence.

Conclusion

The empirical results presented in this chapter illustrate the value of recognizing that there are a variety of concurrences. All concurrences are not the same. Some concurrences support the majority decision, whereas others do not. Some concurrences contract the majority decision, whereas others expand the reach of the majority decision. By merging concurrences and dissents, and by treating concurrences simply as disagreement, important differences and variations among the justices' behavior are lost. The factors that influence a justice's decision whether to write or join a concurrence are different depending on the type of concurrence.

A limiting concurrence is more likely to be written or joined if the justice is a former law professor, if the case is complex, or if the case is legally important. A limiting concurrence is less likely if the case involves a minimum winning coalition, if the justices have a cooperative relationship, if the justice is the chief justice, or if the justice is new to the Court.

An expansive concurrence is more likely when the justice is a former law professor, or if the case is politically or legally salient. An emphatic concurrence is more likely to be written or joined if the case is complex or if the case is politically salient. An emphatic concurrence is less likely when the justices have a cooperative relationship.

A doctrinal concurrence is more likely if the case is complex. It is less likely if the case involves a minimum winning coalition, if the justice is the chief justice, or if the justices have a cooperative relationship. Finally, a reluctant concurrence is less likely if the justice and the majority opinion writer are ideologically compatible.

The decision to write or join a particular type of concurrence is a complex decision that involves justice-specific, case-specific, and institutional factors. The factors that influence a justice's decision whether to write or join a concurrence are different depending on the type of concurrence being written. In the next chapter, I turn to the question of whether concurring opinions result from failed negotiations. In other words, when are efforts at bargaining successful and when do they fail?

3

Potential Concurrences

Insight from Justices Blackmun and Marshall

Bargaining on the merits typically begins after the opinion writer sends the first draft of an opinion to the full Court. From there, the justices who voted with the majority at the initial conference may attempt to bargain over the language of the opinion, including the rationale it invokes and the policy it adopts. The content of opinions is important to the justices and they frequently make concerted efforts to shape the final opinion (see Maltzman, et al. 2000). "[J]ustices care about the development of the law, rather than merely a case's disposition" (Maltzman, et al. 2000, 124).

Justices can bargain in many different ways. They can issue memos in which they make suggestions for opinion revision, describe future action, or explain their action (Epstein and Knight 1998). They also can circulate separate writings. Additionally, more informal bargaining occurs between the clerks acting on behalf of the justices. "Clerks regularly talk to each other about their justices' as well as their own views and positions on cases and issues and then relay that information to their justices" (Ward and Weiden 2006, 159–60).

If their suggestions are not accommodated, the justices may write or join a concurrence. Thus, any bargaining statement is a potential concurrence. If the justice is accommodated, the justice will silently join the majority opinion; however, if the justice is not accommodated, the justice may write or join a concurrence. The concurrence may "outlin[e] the flaws in the majority's legal logic and thus affect ... the future development of the law" (Wahlbeck et al. 1999, 491). As Murphy (1964) explains, "The two major sanctions which a Justice can use against his colleagues are his vote and his willingness to write opinions which will attack a doctrine the ... majority wishes to see adopted" (54).

In this chapter, I use the papers of Justices Harry A. Blackmun and Thurgood Marshall in order to analyze the bargaining and accommodation that occurred during the 1986 to 1989 terms. When are efforts at bargaining successful and when do they fail? Additionally, why are the justices bargaining? Is the justice holding out the threat of a potential concurrence seeking to move the holding in a broader or narrower direction? Is that justice threatening to undermine the majority opinion or simply asking for stylistic changes? By examining the memoranda between the justices and the memoranda of Blackmun's and Marshall's law clerks, this chapter answers these questions.

Bargaining and Accommodation on the Supreme Court

More than forty years ago, Walter Murphy's (1964) classic book, *Elements of Judicial Strategy*, discussed the interactive nature of opinion writing. Murphy argued that Supreme Court justices recognize that their opinions influence public policy and thus can act strategically to have the Court's opinions more closely conform to their policy preferences. To achieve this objective, justices must, at a minimum, take into account the choices made by their colleagues. This may lead justices to bargain and compromise. "For Justices, bargaining is a simple fact of life. Despite conflicting views on literary styles, relevant precedents, procedural rules, and substantive policy, cases have to be settled and opinions written" (57).

Following Murphy's lead and guided by the rational-choice model, Epstein and Knight (1998) gathered aggregate data from justices' personal papers to confirm what Murphy had suggested. The authors argued that relying on "votes" or the attitudinal model to understand Supreme Court behavior is not wrong but rather is incomplete. More is involved than justices responding to ideological values. Assuming the goal is to influence public policy, the justices act strategically toward this goal. To confirm that strategic behavior exists, the authors looked for distinct and discrete evidence that justices are engaged in political choices. The justices' papers were examined for signs of bargaining, thinking ahead, and engaging in sophisticated opinion writing. They found that bargaining is common throughout the process. For example, Epstein and Knight examined the number of times that justices make explicit bargaining statements in judicial memos to other justices. Consistent with Murphy's anecdotally based claims, they found explicit bargaining statements were made quite frequently. In fact, they found that the average case generated six memos, which indicates that justices respond to one another's opinions. In addition, in more than 66 percent of the landmark cases of the 1970s and 1980s, at least one justice tried to strike some sort of bargain with the majority opinion writer. Finally, they compared the policy and rationale adopted in the opinion writer's first circulation with that contained in the published opinion and found that in more than 50 percent of the cases a significant change occurred in the language of the opinion (65% in landmark cases). Thus, Epstein and Knight concluded that the bargaining and accommodation that occurs during the opinion writing process has a "nontrivial effect on the policy the Court ultimately produces" (Epstein and Knight 1998, 106).

Recent work provides empirical, systematic evidence that the justices play the "collegial game"[1] in an effort to shape the content of opinions (Maltzman, et al. 2000). The authors, relying on the available files of Justice William Brennan, generated their data from assignment sheets, docket sheets, and circulated records. From these materials, they developed a database to assess their collegial model of Supreme Court decision making. The authors used the data to show that "[j]ustices will try to secure opinions that are as close as possible to their policy positions by basing their decisions in part on the positions and actions of their colleagues" (Maltzman, et al. 2000, 17).

Specifically, they found that justices are more likely to bargain with the majority opinion author if they are either ideologically removed from the author or the supporting coalition, if the author had previously been extremely uncooperative with a justice, and when the conference coalition is smaller.[2] The majority opinion author is more likely to accommodate (as measured by the decision to circulate additional drafts) when he is ideologically farther away from those majority conference coalition justices not having joined the opinion or if the nonjoiners are ideologically heterogeneous. Additionally, the likelihood of the author circulating an additional draft opinion decreases for larger conference majorities, and, once at least a majority of justices have joined the majority opinion, authors are less likely to accommodate.[3] Finally, the authors found that a justice's final decision to join an opinion is influenced by his or her policy goals, but the timing and willingness of the decision to join the majority opinion varies along with the changing size of the majority opinion coalition, the different bargaining tactics used by the other justices, and the cooperative relationship each justice has with each of his or her colleagues.

Bargaining and Accommodation: Insight from the Chambers of Justices Blackmun and Marshall

The information in this section comes from the private papers of Blackmun and Marshall. I examined memos between Blackmun and Marshall and the other justices, and the memos of Blackmun and Marshall's law clerks in order to gain insight into the bargaining and accommodation that occurred between Blackmun and Marshall and the other justices, which culminated in a final, published opinion.[4]

During the 1986 to 1989 terms, Blackmun authored fifty-five majority opinions.[5] Of those cases, thirty-one (56%) contained at least one bargaining statement from another justice.[6] Of those thirty-one cases, Blackmun made some sort of accommodation in twenty-eight cases (90%).[7] Of those cases, in only six (21%) did the negotiations between the justices fail, resulting in a published concurrence. Thus, in twenty-two cases (79%), the justices successfully bargained and accommodated. Interestingly, in five cases, there were no attempts at bargaining by any of the justices; however, a justice did publish a concurrence. Perhaps the concurring justice, based on the discussion at the initial conference or based on his past dealings with Blackmun, knew his suggested changes would not be made.

During the 1986 to 1989 terms, Marshall authored fifty-eight majority opinions. Of those cases, thirty-seven (64%) contained at least one bargaining statement from another justice. Of the thirty-seven cases, Marshall made some sort of accommodation in thirty (81%). Consistent with the findings by other scholars, there is a good deal of bargaining and accommodation that takes place and it is a regular practice by which justices reach their decisions.

Which justices attempted to bargain with Blackmun or Marshall over the content of the final opinion and which ones did the justices accommodate? Table 3.1 displays the results of the bargaining and accommodation between Blackmun and Marshall and their colleagues.

Kennedy, Scalia, and Powell were more likely to bargain with Blackmun, whereas Scalia, O'Connor, and Powell were more likely to bargain with Marshall over the content of the majority opinion. Interestingly, Marshall never attempted to bargain with Blackmun and Blackmun only attempted to bargain with Marshall in two cases. After Marshall, White and Brennan were the least likely to bargain with Blackmun, whereas Brennan did not bargain very often with Marshall, and attempted to bargain with him in only five out of fifty-six cases (9%).

Brennan and Powell were the most successful at bargaining with Blackmun, whereas Blackmun and Powell were the most successful at bargaining with Marshall, with both justices accommodating to some extent all of their suggestions. Scalia also had a high rate of success at bargaining with Blackmun, with 93 percent of his suggestions accommodated and Rehnquist had a high rate of success with Marshall, with 90 percent of his suggestions accommodated. Although Kennedy was the least successful of the justices to successfully negotiate with Blackmun, Blackmun still accommodated 60 percent of his suggestions. Although O'Connor and Scalia were the least successful at negotiating with Marshall, 71 percent of their suggestions were still accommodated.

Thus, the data indicate a substantial amount of successful bargaining takes place on the Supreme Court. The next section describes that successful bargaining.

Table 3.1. Bargaining and Accommodation Between Blackmun and Marshall and the Other Justices, 1986–1989 Terms

| | Blackmun ||| Marshall |||
Justice	No. of Cases Justice in Majority	No. of Cases Bargaining Occurred	No. of Cases Accommodation Occurred	No. of Cases Justice in Majority	No. of Cases Bargaining Occurred	No. of Cases Accommodation Occurred
Marshall	40	0 (0%)	0 (0%)	—	—	—
Brennan	41	6 (15%)	6 (100%)	56	5 (9%)	4 (80%)
White	44	6 (14%)	4 (67%)	49	12 (24%)	9 (75%)
Powell	12	4 (33%)	4 (100%)	14	4 (29%)	4 (100%)
Rehnquist	41	10 (24%)	7 (70%)	47	10 (21%)	9 (90%)
Stevens	39	8 (21%)	7 (87.5%)	49	8 (16%)	7 (88%)
O'Connor	39	7 (18%)	7 (100%)	43	14 (33%)	10 (71%)
Scalia	44	15 (34%)	14 (93%)	44	17 (39%)	12 (71%)
Kennedy	28	10 (36%)	6 (60%)	28	6 (21%)	5 (83%)
Blackmun	—	—	—	51	2 (4%)	2 (100%)

Potential Concurrences: Successful Negotiations

In *R.J. Reynolds v. Durham County* (1986), the issue was whether Congress had exercised its power under the Supremacy Clause[8] to preempt ad valorem state taxation of imported goods that were being stored in customs-bonded warehouses and destined for domestic markets. Scalia wrote a memo to Blackmun[9] requesting a few modifications to the draft opinion. The first modification was as follows:

> I do not want to pronounce on whether taxes may be assessed but deferred with regard to goods held in a warehouse for indeterminate destination. Nor on what degree of indeterminateness must exist in order to prevent annual collection of taxes. . . . Neither of these issues is presented in the case. Thus, I would urge revision of footnote 17.

The second request from Scalia related to his views on statutory interpretation. "I think it understates the matter to say that interpretations of an earlier statute by a later Congress legislating on a different subject 'are not conclusive.' I would most prefer 'are not persuasive.'"

Third, Scalia wrote: "It seems to me that when regulations validly preempt state law, they do so not precisely because of a congressional desire to preempt, but because of a congressional desire to permit the agent to preempt. I would favor deleting the phrase 'on the part of Congress' in line 13 of the text" (Blackmun 1986a).

Blackmun then received a memo from his law clerk, offering his comments on Scalia's memos.

> I am not surprised that he has focused on footnote 17, because this footnote does anticipate future cases. It is somewhat unfortunate, however, that he did not circulate this note to the entire conference. I put in the note, as you know, because some members of the Court, particularly Justice O'Connor, wanted some language suggesting how we might come out on the cases in the "middle." If Justice Scalia's memorandum had been circulated to everybody, then Justice O'Connor and others might be alerted to his position (unannounced in conference) and might respond to it accordingly (i.e., for all we know, she might agree). As it is, we are in the position of having to wait for the other votes to see how the remaining members of the majority react to the language without the benefit of Justice Scalia's observations, which

are not without force. And, I suppose, we shall have to decide whom we most want to join the opinion.

The clerk's memo went on to state that he had no problem with the second suggestion but that he was a little troubled by the third.

> Originally, I had hoped to formulate a sentence to emphasize more the agency's action in the preemption, but the cites seemed more to focus on Congress' desire, as evidenced by agency action. We might be splitting hairs here. In any event, the deletion proposed by Scalia leaves the attribution of the word "desire" somewhat up in the air (is it Congress' desire? Or an agency's?). Perhaps that ambiguity is useful, for it satisfies Scalia and could still be interpreted as linking desire to Congress. (Blackmun 1986b)

The next day, Blackmun wrote a memo to Stevens and O'Connor, letting them know about Scalia's suggestion regarding footnote 17. "I wrote footnote 17 as originally circulated because of what my notes indicated were your respective comments at conference. I could go along with Nino's suggestion provided that it meets with your approval. If either of you does not approve, I shall tell him that footnote 17 will remain as it is. Would you let me know?" (Blackmun 1986c).

O'Connor wrote Blackmun, explaining that she thought footnote 17 was correct, but she would not stand in his way if he wanted to accept Scalia's suggestion (Blackmun 1986d). Blackmun then wrote to Scalia:

> Your second and third suggestions did not bother me, and I am glad to make those minor changes. Your first suggestion was more troublesome, for I drafted footnote 17 as I did because of comments made by John and Sandra at conference. I did not wish, by incorporating your suggestion as to footnote 17, to upset their votes, so I submitted your proposal to them. I enclose copies of their respective responses. While I—and·I assume they—would prefer footnote 17 as originally drafted, you apparently are distinctly uncomfortable with it. Therefore, to ease your discomfort, I shall adopt your suggestion in the hope that by doing so we shall have a unanimous Court on this case. (Blackmun 1986e)

Scalia then sent the following memo:

> Many thanks for your changes. In view of the expressed preferences of you, Sandra and John, I revisited footnote 17, but I remain,

as you well expressed it, "distinctly uncomfortable" with the prior version. By a separate memorandum to you, I am advising the Conference of my desire to join your opinion. Thank you once again. (Blackmun 1986f)

Thus, in this case, there were three suggestions made by Scalia. Two were relatively minor; however, if Blackmun had not accommodated Scalia, he could have written a brief concurrence. The third suggestion regarding footnote 17 was one that, if Scalia's change had not been adopted, would have led to a limiting concurrence because the opinion would have addressed issues that Scalia felt were not presented in the case. What is interesting about this footnote is that it was written to preemptively accommodate (see Maltzman, et al. 2000) O'Connor and Stevens based on comments they made at conference. It also is interesting that Scalia chose not to circulate this memo to the entire conference, instead sending the memo with the requested change only to Blackmun. This move by Scalia put the ball in Blackmun's court, so to speak, for he had to decide how best to respond to Scalia's memo. Blackmun chose to let O'Connor and Stevens know what was going on, and decided that if they did not approve of the change, he would leave the footnote as it was originally drafted, and Scalia more than likely would have written a concurrence. From the memos that were circulated in this case, it is clear that the opinion writer has to take into account the other members of the majority coalition when another justice is requesting a substantive modification. Because the other justices did not insist on the original draft, Blackmun was able to completely accommodate Scalia's request, and successfully prevent a concurrence.

Another case in which Blackmun had to take into account the other members of the majority coalition is *Pinter v. Dahl* (1988), which involved the Securities Act of 1933. Scalia made a number of suggested changes to the majority draft. According to Blackmun's clerk:

> I think we can accommodate most of Justice Scalia's concerns, . . . I do not think that there is any substantive disagreement between you and Justice Scalia, and to the extent his suggestions clarify our position, I think we should welcome them. Frankly, I think he is being overly cautious, but, as long as our adopting his suggestions are not interpreted by others (in particular WJB and TM)[10] as narrowing liability even farther, I don't suppose there is any harm in taking the more cautious route. (Blackmun 1988a)

Blackmun substantially accommodated Scalia's requests, and Scalia joined the opinion.

Marshall's papers also provide some insight into how the justices have to take into account the other members of the majority coalition. In *Burlington Northern v. Woods*, (1987), the Court was faced with a state statute requiring a mandatory 10 percent penalty when the trial court enters a money judgment or decree, the judgment or decree is stayed by requisite bond, and the judgment or decree is affirmed without substantial modification. The purposes of the mandatory affirmance penalty are to penalize frivolous appeals and to provide additional damages as compensation to the appellees for having to defend the judgment on appeal. Jurisdiction in federal court was based on diversity. Rule 38 of the Federal Rules of Appellate procedure provides: "If the court of appeals shall determine that an appeal is frivolous, it may award just damages." Under this Rule, "damages are awarded by the court in its discretion."

In the first draft of the majority opinion, Part II analyzed the issue under the *Hanna* analysis,[11] and Part III handled the case as a Rules of Decision case.[12] According to Marshall's law clerk:

> There is complete unanimity on the result, but quite a bit of disagreement on how to get there. One possibility is to stop at the end of Part II, discussing only *Hanna*.... [T]he second possibility is to ignore *Hanna* altogether and handle the case as a Rules of Decision case. I think some discussion of this approach is needed, so Part III has been included. (Marshall 1987a)

Brennan sent a memo to Marshall, expressing his desire that the case should be decided under the *Hanna* analysis.

> This is an important case because the *Hanna* test has not been used previously to strike down a state law. The *Hanna* analysis is more appropriate than the *Erie* analysis in this case because the *Hanna* test specifically safeguards the federal policies underlying the Federal Rules. Here I find a direct conflict between the federal rules and a state procedural rule which, in effect, penalizes the defendant's right to appeal. I favor striking down this state procedural rule because of the federal interest in the integrity and uniformity of the federal appellate system far outweighs any state interest in imposing a discriminatory rule upon the federal courts. I could join your opinion if you simply completed the *Hanna* analysis in Part II. Part III would then be unnecessary to decide this case. (Marshall 1987b)

In Marshall's response to Brennan's memo, although he was open to suggestions for strengthening Part II, he was not convinced that Part III was unnecessary. Three days later, he received a memo from Powell, in which Powell expressed concern "over what seems to me to be the alternative lines of decision in Parts II and III." Specifically, he stated the following:

> I have thought we could decide [this case] in a straightforward manner by relying on the conflict between the federal Rules, specifically Rule 38, and the Alabama affirmance Penalty statute.... In sum, I will certainly join your judgment, and will write a brief concurring opinion. (Marshall 1987c)

The next day, Brennan wrote a memo to Marshall, stating: "My view appears to coincide with Lewis' approach [and I] will await Lewis' concurring opinion" (Marshall 1987d). Marshall's law clerk then wrote him a memo, stating that "[i]t may be time for a judgment call on this case. LFP, WJB and HAB appear set on accepting only the *Hanna* analysis contained in Part II of the draft opinion."[13] The clerk further wrote:

> There is a good chance that if we respond to LFP immediately with, "I can go along and, assuming no objection from those who have already joined ... will shortly circulate a revised draft relying solely on the *Hanna* analysis," that LFP will not write separately but will join. (His law clerk indicates LFP would prefer not to write, but did not feel comfortable asking for such a substantial revision as a condition of his vote.) (Marshall 1987e)

That same day, Marshall wrote the following memo to Brennan and Powell, which he also sent to the rest of the conference: "I plan to circulate a revised opinion in this case taking into account your preferences in the *Hanna* analysis" (Marshall 1987f). Marshall ended up deleting Part III from the opinion, and the majority opinion was supported by a unanimous vote, with no concurrences written.

Although the justices are members of the majority coalition, and agree with the outcome of the decision, the majority opinion writer is still concerned with gaining five votes for the reasoning and rationale behind the decision. "[N]o opinion may carry the institutional label of the Court unless five Justices agree to sign it" (Murphy 1964, 57). In fact, the majority opinion writer is concerned with at least five votes for the *entire* opinion. In *Omni v. Wolff* (1987), the issue involved personal jurisdiction over the defendant corporation, specifically service of process.[14] O'Connor wrote a memo to Blackmun, joining him in all but footnote 10 of his opinion. "I am not inclined to invite challenges to the *Robertson* holding" (Blackmun 1987a).[15] Three days later, Rehnquist sent a memo to Blackmun, joining the opinion, but expressing his preference that the footnote be changed the way O'Connor suggested. However, he did not make his join conditional on the change (Blackmun 1987b).

Blackmun's clerk then wrote a memo regarding footnote 10. "I talked to WJB's clerk about footnote 10. His impression of what WJB thinks about note 10 is that WJB certainly would prefer that it remain in the opinion, but, if push came to shove, they might not write separately if we deleted it. He said he thought WJB would be amenable to a watered down version of the footnote." Thus, the clerk expressed concern that Brennan would write a concurrence with respect to this footnote. The clerk then suggested a change to the footnote. "These changes would do two things. First, the note would not suggest that *Robertson's* rule no longer has force (after all we ultimately reach the same conclusion as *Robertson*), but only that its reasoning no longer has force. Second, by changing the 'was' to a 'may have been,' we reach absolutely no conclusions in the footnote" (Blackmun 1987c).

Blackmun then received a memo from Scalia, also joining all of the opinion except for footnote 10 (Blackmun 1987d). Blackmun then circulated a second draft of the opinion, changing footnote 10. "The revised form may or may not be acceptable to you. If it is, please let me know" (Blackmun 1987e). O'Connor then withdrew her objection (Blackmun 1987f) and Scalia then joined the opinion "in its entirety" (Blackmun 1987g). Thus, Blackmun accommodated in order to get the justices to join his *entire* opinion, including the footnote.

Another example is found in *Kentucky Dept. of Corrections v. Thompson* (1989). The issue in this case was whether Kentucky prison regulations gave state inmates, for purposes of the Fourteenth Amendment, a liberty interest in receiving certain visitors. Rehnquist wrote to Blackmun, expressing reservations about footnote 3, which created a bright-line rule. This rule stated that prison regulations, regardless of the mandatory character of their language or the extent to which they limited official discretion, "do not create an entitlement protected by the Due Process Clause when they do not affect the duration or release from confinement, or the very nature of confinement." He wished to leave the question open for future development. He stated that he "see[s] no reason to reject an argument which we need not even reach." Thus, Rehnquist wished to limit the reach of the opinion. He further wrote: "If you can find some way to modify the footnote in this direction, I will be happy to join the entire opinion. If not, show me as joining all but footnote 3" (Blackmun 1989a). Blackmun agreed to the change, and Rehnquist joined the opinion in its entirety.

Sometimes the majority opinion writer is pulled in two different directions by the justices.

> The Justice who has been assigned the task of writing the opinion of the Court may see himself as a broker adjusting the interests of his associates as well as of himself. His problems, of course, are dynamic rather than static. By making a change in an opinion to pick up one vote he may lose another. (Murphy 1964, 64)

In *United States v. Zolin* (1989), a case that arose out of efforts of the IRS to investigate the tax returns of L. Ron Hubbard, the founder of the Church of Scientology, Kennedy wrote to Blackmun, expressing his concern over Blackmun's articulation of a rule to guide district courts as to when they may examine documents alleged to fall under the crime-fraud exception to the attorney–client privilege.[16] The original draft stated that the trial court "should require a showing of a factual basis adequate to support a good faith belief by a reasonable person that *in camera* review of the materials will reveal evidence to support the claim that the crime-fraud exception applies." Kennedy read this to be a stringent standard, whereas he thought that district court judges should be allowed greater latitude. He then suggested that the "will" be changed to "may." The required showing would then be "a factual basis adequate to support a good faith belief by a reasonable person that *in camera* review of the materials *may* reveal evidence to support the claim that the crime-fraud exception applies" (Blackmun 1989b).

Blackmun wrote to Kennedy, agreeing to the change (Blackmun 1989c). He then received a memo from Scalia, noting that the opinion described the test twice. The first was the time that Kennedy's memo referred to but then later the opinion stated that the test was a reasonable belief that *in camera* review "may yield further evidence in support of the exception's applicability." Scalia noted that "evidence to support the claim" could be taken to mean "evidence sufficient to establish the claim" but that "further evidence in support of" the claim fell far short of that. He suggested that the privilege should not be set aside unless "there is a reasonable belief that the communication in question may (together with other evidence, of course) establish the crime-fraud exception. I would prefer using that very word." Scalia agreed to join the opinion, if the change was made. However, he explained that if the change was not made, "I will write the briefest of concurrences, expressing the point made above" (Blackmun 1989d).

Blackmun then wrote a memo to Scalia, in which he expressed his feeling that he was "being pulled one way by Tony and another way by you." He proposed a partial accommodation to Scalia's suggestion. "This probably is not enough for you, so you may feel that you must concur separately" (Blackmun 1989e). Scalia wrote back, stating that the proposition did not solve his difficulty; it even made it worse. He then stated his intention to write separately (Blackmun 1989f). In the meantime, apparently at Blackmun's request, Scalia and Kennedy got together to see if they could agree on a proposal for the articulation of the standard that should govern in the case. Kennedy wrote a memo to Blackmun with the changes they had both agreed to, which solved the problem (Blackmun 1989g). Blackmun then wrote a memo to the entire conference: "Nino and Tony have been able to get together to reach an agreement as to their initial differences. This draft, to the extent that I can, accommodates what they have agreed upon" (Blackmun 1989h). Both Scalia and Kennedy joined the opinion, with no published concurrences. Although Blackmun was not able to accommodate Scalia and Kennedy himself, they were able to work it out together and accommodate one another.

Basic v. Levinson (1988) provides another example of successful negotiation. In this case, one of the issues involved whether a person who trades a corporation's shares on a securities exchange after the issuance of a materially misleading statement by the corporation may invoke a rebuttable presumption that, in trading, he relied on the integrity of the price set by the market. Stevens expressed two minor concerns; however, his joining the opinion was unconditional (Blackmun 1988b). Blackmun agreed to the changes. Blackmun then received a memo from Brennan, in which he stated he had problems with Part IV of the opinion regarding the fraud on the market theory[17] (Blackmun 1988c). Blackmun attempted to alleviate his concerns by explaining his reasoning for the opinion. Brennan thanked him for his response, but was still concerned over that part of the opinion. "I appreciate the difficulty in meeting my concerns without risking the loss of John's vote. Perhaps there is some common ground that we can all reach" (Blackmun 1988d).

Blackmun responded with a few changes. "This, I fear, is about the best I can do to respond to the concern you have outlined at such length. I shall be glad to make the indicated changes if they are of assistance" (Blackmun 1988e). Brennan responded:

> I think we've about exhausted all either of us need to say in this case. The difference between us is now clear. In my view, the market relies on the defendant's misstatement, and plaintiffs are defrauded because they are forced to act through the market. Your view requires that in addition plaintiffs specifically depend on the integrity of the market, that is, that the market is fair. This difference of opinion, I must agree, will have little, if any, effect on the outcome of section 10(b) cases. If, as I suspect, defendants find it impractical to utilize the rebuttal option, and if the measure of damages is ultimately resolved as the difference between the price actually received and the price that would have been received had the market been fair, my view and your

view will lead to identical results, although by somewhat different routes. Consequently, any writing separately by me would serve no purpose save to confuse the lower courts unnecessarily. Therefore, I think I should join your opinion in its entirety. I do so with pleasure. (Blackmun 1988f)

Thus, in this case, Brennan could have chosen to write a concurrence; however, he decided that to do so would only serve to confuse the lower courts while the result would still be the same. Had Brennan only been concerned with the vote or outcome in the case he would not have issued the memoranda in the first place. Had he solely been concerned with expressing his own view of the law he would not have ultimately decided against writing separately. In short, Brennan's concern for clarity in the law trumped his individual disagreement with Blackmun.

When more than one justice wanted a particular change, it seems that Blackmun and Marshall were more likely to accommodate them. In *Thornburgh v. Abbott* (1989), regulations promulgated by the Federal Bureau of Prisons permitted federal prisoners to receive publications from the outside, but authorized prison officials to reject incoming publications that were found to be detrimental to institutional security. Inmates and publishers claimed that these regulations violated their First Amendment rights under the standard of review enunciated in *Procunier v. Martinez* (1974). In *Martinez*, the Court struck down California regulations concerning personal correspondence between inmates and non-inmates, reviewing the regulations under the following standard:

> First, the regulation or practice in question must further an important or substantial government interest unrelated to the suppression of expression. Prison officials ... must show that a regulation authorizing mail censorship furthers one or more of the substantial governmental interests of security, order, and rehabilitation. Second, the limitation of First Amendment freedoms must be no greater than is necessary or essential to the protection of the particular governmental interest involved. Thus a restriction on inmate correspondence that furthers an important or substantial interest of penal administration will nevertheless be invalid if its sweep is unnecessarily broad. (*Martinez* 1974, 413–14)

In Blackmun's first draft, he upheld the regulations, distinguishing the case from *Martinez*. White wrote a memo to Blackmun, stating: "I'm not sure where your draft leaves *Martinez*. But I shall likely be with you unless there is other writing expressing a cleaner break with *Martinez*, in which event

I would want to consider that view" (Blackmun 1989i). Rehnquist then sent Blackmun a memo, expressing agreement with White. "Like Byron, I had hoped that this case could be used to limit *Martinez* more than your circulating draft would do. I think that under the principles you enumerate in your draft—with which I fully agree—*Martinez* should be limited to outgoing correspondence. Even if you prefer not to decide that in this case, it seems to me that the question should be at least left open." He then suggested some changes to the opinion. "If you can make these changes, or ones accomplishing substantially the same result, I will be happy to join" (Blackmun 1989j).

Scalia sent a memo to Blackmun, in which he also agreed with White. "Though, like Byron, I would prefer to overrule *Martinez*, I can with one exception go along with your careful distinguishing of it." He then suggested a modification of footnote 11 (Blackmun 1989k).

Blackmun then responded to the memos:

> My conference notes are not very helpful as to whether any decision was made concerning the treatment of *Martinez*. Certainly, at that time a majority did not express a desire to overrule *Martinez* in its entirety. At least two of you appear to be ready to take that step now. My notes also do not clearly disclose whether there would be a majority to cut back on *Martinez* by confining its application to outgoing mail. In an endeavor to bring this to a head, I am circulating a second draft. It is generally responsive to the Chief's and Nino's suggestions, but not entirely so because they are in partial disagreement. What I have done, however, at the end of Part III of the opinion, is to state flatly that any *Martinez* precedent is confined to outgoing mail. I am willing to take that step, and I suspect that the three of you would do so, too. (Blackmun 1989l)

Because three justices wanted the opinion to limit or even overrule a particular case, Blackmun, although not agreeing to overrule the case, did limit its application rather than distinguishing it. The memos circulated in this case also show how the majority opinion writer preemptively accommodates the views expressed at the conference. In this case, Blackmun's notes were not clear on this issue; thus, he was not able to preemptively accommodate their concerns, which led to the suggested changes. If those changes had not been made, more than likely the three justices would have written a concurrence expressing their views regarding limiting or overruling *Martinez*.

Another case in which more than one justice wanted a particular change was *Adams Fruit Co. v. Barrett* (1990). In *Adams Fruit Co.*, the issue was whether exclusivity provisions in state workers' compensation laws barred migrant workers from bringing suit under the Migrant and Seasonal Agricultural Worker Protection Act.[18] After Marshall circulated his first draft, O'Connor wrote a memo in which she expressed concerns with the first draft. Specifically, "[t]he opinion adopts several presumptions which I am inclined to think are unnecessary and unwarranted." Based on those concerns, she informed Marshall that she intended to write separately, although she agreed with the result (Marshall 1990a). Scalia then wrote a memo in which he expressed problems with the opinion that prevented him from joining and stated that he would wait for O'Connor's concurrence. First, he wrote:

> I do not recall petitioner's making the argument that, "where Congress authorizes a private right of action to vindicate a federal right, we should generally presume that Congress intends to withdraw the right of action where an alternative state remedy is available." If the argument was made, it is so absurd that it should not be dignified with refutation. If we do refute it, however, I am not sure I agree that there is an opposite "presumption." Federal rights supplement state-created rights unless otherwise indicated. If that is what you mean by a "presumption" I guess I agree, but it seems strange to call it a presumption. In any case, I do not agree that the "presumption" (if one calls it that) "may be overcome only by clear, express language to the contrary." It seems to me that this entire discussion needlessly leads us into difficult terrain.

Scalia also expressed the following problem with the first draft:

> I do not think that an issue of federal "pre-emption" of state law is created by a state law that purports to eliminate the effect of a federal statute (here, supposedly, the Florida workers' comp exclusivity provision). Rather, I would describe that as an issue of state "pre-emption" of federal law—which is easily resolved by saying that there is no such thing. Whatever there was to petitioner's "failure to pre-empt exclusivity" argument could easily have been answered by saying that there is no reason to believe Florida's exclusivity provision was directed at federal law, and that if it was it would be unconstitutional. Once again, I think we needlessly traverse difficult terrain. (Marshall 1990b)

The next day, White sent a memo to Marshall, agreeing with most of Scalia's views (Marshall 1990c). At this point, three justices were requesting modifications to the opinion and Marshall circulated a second draft in an attempt to accommodate them. After he circulated this draft, Kennedy wrote him a memo, expressing agreement with White, Scalia, and O'Connor. "Your second draft retains much of the earlier material I thought troubling, so I think I must await Sandra's writing" (Marshall 1990d). Marshall then received a memo from Rehnquist, who shared the concerns expressed by the other justices, which prevented him from joining the second draft (Marshall 1990e). Marshall then wrote and circulated a third draft and all of the justices joined the opinion. Specifically, O'Connor wrote: "The revisions contained in your 3rd draft meet the bulk of my concerns, and I am pleased to join it. I will not circulate my separate writing" (Marshall 1990f).

In *Quinn v. Millsap* (1989), the issue was whether a Missouri constitutional provision, which provided that the governments of the city of St. Louis and St. Louis County may be reorganized by a vote of the electorate of the city and county on a plan of reorganization drafted by a "board of freeholders," violated the Equal Protection Clause because it required every member of the board to own real property. Blackmun's law clerk, based on notes from the conference and from talking with other law clerks, drafted the opinion to avoid the as-applied challenge[19] to the Equal Protection Clause as much as possible, "especially because this case is supposed to be unanimous" (Blackmun 1989m). After the draft was circulated, Kennedy expressed his general agreement with the opinion, with the exception of the last paragraph of footnote 9,

> which suggests that appellants' as-applied challenge is properly before us. In footnote 8, the opinion declines to address the question whether appellants have standing to bring an as-applied challenge, on the ground that they have standing to raise their facial challenge. Since the opinion's resolution of the facial challenge is sufficient to decide this case, and the as-applied challenge raises somewhat more difficult issues, I would prefer to avoid any discussion of the as-applied challenge. (Blackmun 1989n)

In short, Kennedy wished to limit the majority opinion's discussion to the facial challenge only.

Blackmun's clerk advised him as follows:

> AMK has asked you to remove the last paragraph of n. 9 because it relates to the as-applied issue. I think he is being overly finicky. The point about Father Reinhert may relate to the as-applied challenge, but it is also strong support for the Court's assumption that land ownership was required of all members. However, the

opinion is careful not to say (as even AMK acknowledges) that appellants have standing to bring an as-applied claim. Rather, having concluded that appellants have standing to bring their appeal, and it being necessary to assume the existence of a real property requirement in order to decide the rationality issue on this appeal, this paragraph simply adds an additional reason to support the necessary assumption. Thus, I would prefer that the opinion retain this paragraph, but I also don't think it would be especially harmful to remove it. I don't think it is something worth fighting over. Of course, you already have a Court without AMK, but there is always the possibility that the Chief or SOC will agree with AMK's suggestion (Who knows what BRW will do, but I'm sure AS will agree with AMK on this point.) In sum, I guess my inclination is to give in on this one, although I think it is unfortunate that AMK objected to this useful paragraph. (Blackmun 1989o).

Even though Blackmun's clerk advised him to accommodate Kennedy's suggestion, Blackmun declined to do so, explaining: "It seems to me that it affords additional support for the Court's assumption that land ownership was required of all members, and we are careful not to say (I thought) that appellants have standing to bring an as-applied claim" (Blackmun 1989p).

The next day, Blackmun received a memo from Scalia, in which he joined the opinion; however, he agreed with Kennedy's suggestion regarding footnote 9. He also suggested another change to the same footnote:

> It does not seem to me we should make it excessively embarrassing for the Missouri Supreme Court to adopt whatever interpretation of the Missouri Constitution it pleases—as I think we do by describing the validating interpretation as "an unusual feat of judicial ingenuity." I think our point would be well enough established by saying instead that . . . "we have no substantial reason to believe that appellee's interpretation might be accepted."

Scalia concluded by stating that he would go along with Blackmun's judgment on both of his suggestions (Blackmun 1989q). Blackmun agreed to Scalia's second suggestion. Unlike *Thornbugh v. Abbott*, even though two justices wanted the same change, Blackmun did not accommodate them. However, Kennedy did not write a concurrence, perhaps accepting Blackmun's explanation.

In *Blanton v. North Las Vegas* (1989), a case that involved whether there is a constitutional right to a trial by jury for individuals charged with driving under the influence of alcohol, Marshall wrote the first draft and received a suggestion from Kennedy that footnote 9 be changed "because I think it may give more weight to the 90-day license suspension than is warranted"[20] (Marshall 1989a). White then wrote a memo, stating: "I join your opinion but suggest that the last sentence of the first paragraph of footnote 7 be replaced with the following: 'That statement, however, dealt only with cases involving prison or jail sentences'" (Marshall 1989b). Rehnquist then sent the following memo to Marshall: "If you can see your way clear to accommodate the suggestions of Bryon and Tony I will be happy to join" (Marshall 1989c).

Marshall responded, agreeing to accommodate White's suggestion, but only partially accommodating Kennedy's suggestion.

> With respect to footnote 9 on page 6, I cannot agree with Tony's proposed third sentence. It could be read to suggest that nonincarceration penalties can never give rise to a jury trial when the maximum authorized jail term is six months or less—a proposition the rest of the opinion does not endorse. I have, however decided to include a citation to Frank. I hope these changes adequately address your concerns. (Marshall 1989d)

Even though Marshall only partially accommodated Kennedy's suggestion, Rehnquist and Kennedy both joined Marshall's opinion, and Kennedy wrote: "I suppose half a loaf (or even a single slice) is better than none. Please join me" (Marshall 1989e).

Unsuccessful Negotiations

There were cases in which justices attempted to bargain with Blackmun and Marshall over the content of the opinions, but the bargaining failed and, consequently, a concurrence was written. One example from the Blackmun papers is *Gray v. Mississippi* (1987), a case involving the death penalty. In order to understand the memos between the justices, a little background is necessary. In *Witherspoon v. Illinois* (1968), the Court held that a state statute providing grounds for the dismissal of any juror with "conscientious scruples" against capital punishment violated the Sixth Amendment's guarantee of an "impartial jury." The Court held that although jurors who say they will not impose the death penalty can be dismissed, jurors who simply oppose the death penalty as a personal belief may not. In a later case, *Davis v. Georgia* (1976), the Court ruled that when a trial court misapplies *Witherspoon* and excludes from a capital jury a prospective juror who in fact is qualified to serve, a death sentence cannot stand. The *Witherspoon* rule was reexamined in *Wainwright v. Witt* (1985), and the Court clarified the standard for determining whether prospective jurors may be excluded for cause based on their views on capital punishment. In *Wainwright*, the Court held that the relevant inquiry is "whether the juror's views would 'prevent or substantially impair the performance of his duties as a juror in accordance with his instructions and his oath'" (*Wainwright* 1985, 424).

The question in *Gray* was whether the Court should abandon that ruling and subject an impermissible exclusion to harmless-error review.[21] Powell wrote Blackmun a memo, agreeing with the judgment and much of the opinion, but expressing some concerns.

> On p. 18, you suggest that it would violate both *Witherspoon* and *Witt* for a prosecutor to use his peremptory challenges[22] to remove all panel members "who express any degree of uneasiness about learning that the state intends to seek the death penalty." I am not sure that I understand the foregoing. In *Adams v. Texas*, 448 U.S. 38, we restated the *Witherspoon* standard for determining juror exclusion. And in *Wainwright v. Witt*, we expressly modified *Witherspoon*, and adopted the *Adams* standard. The question under it is whether the juror's concerns as to capital punishment would "prevent or substantial[ly] impair the performance of his duties as a juror in accordance with his instructions and his oath." 469 U.S., at 424. I would agree that in this case, because of the apparent incompetence of the trial judge, it is not clear what standard, if any, was applied. On the basis of the TC's initial rulings, the prosecutor used most of his peremptory challenges to remove panel members who he thought should have been excused for cause. The TC subsequently agreed that five of these should have been excused for cause (your opinion, p. 5), but nevertheless refused to change his ruling. Instead, he made the error of excluding Bounds, a panel member who was obviously qualified. I think it is settled by our cases ... that jurors may be excused for cause whenever it is clear that his or her views as to capital punishment would "impair the performance of his duties as a juror." It would be error, of course, for a TC to exclude for cause a juror whose view met the *Witt* standard. But we have never held that the prosecutor had no right to excuse such a potential juror by the exercise of a peremptory challenge. I am concerned that the language on page 18 of your opinion can be read to deny this right.

Powell then brought up two points that were "not as important" (Blackmun 1987h).

One of Blackmun's clerks wrote a memo addressing Powell's letter. She thought that Powell's observation that the discussion of peremptory challenges could be read more broadly than intended was plausible. However, she admitted: "[M]y conclusion that his observation is not unreasonable is influenced by the fact that he would be a fifth vote to make the opinion a majority rather than a plurality." Thus, she stated:

> [i]f Justice Powell would join the opinion with some modifications, I think it would be well worth it to make such modifications. Again, however, I do not think that you should go as far as Justice Powell does in his letter and state that in addition to being able to remove *Witherspoon/Witt* excludables, prosecutors have a right to peremptorily strike jurors on the basis of their views on the death penalty. That question is not presented here. (Blackmun 1987i)

On the basis of the memo written by Blackmun's law clerk, it is clear that Blackmun might have chosen to accommodate Powell because he would have been the fifth vote.[23] "[G]iven the high value of these first four votes, [the opinion writer] should rationally be willing to pay a relatively high price in accommodation to secure them" (Murphy 1964, 65). However, that did not mean that Powell's suggestion would be completely accommodated if the price was too high.

Blackmun then wrote a letter to Powell, proposing changes to accommodate his concerns. Powell replied that he "continue[s] to be concerned . . . by your reliance on the multiple peremptory challenges." Powell believed that because Bounds was improperly excluded, it was unnecessary to do more than reaffirm *Davis*.

> I continue to be troubled, therefore, by the suggestion that it is relevant to our decision that the prosecutor exercised his "peremptory challenges to remove all venire members who expressed any degree of hesitation against the death penalty." This may be read as indicating that our analysis in Batson[24] somehow extends to the prosecutor's use of peremptory challenges. I would have to give this considerable thought in a proper case, but this question is not presented in this case. Raising it as a possibility would invite new habeas corpus applications in capital cases, perhaps in substantial numbers.

Powell asked Blackmun to remove the discussion of the prosecutor's use of peremptory challenges, as well as two footnotes (Blackmun 1987j).

Almost two months passed with no correspondence. Powell then wrote to Blackmun, stating that he would join the judgment in order to assure him a Court. In a memo to Blackmun, his clerk explained that she "agree[s] with your decision not to accommodate his request that you remove the discussion of the prosecutor's actual use of peremptory challenges in this case" (Blackmun 1987k).

Blackmun wrote a memo to Powell, expressing disappointment that his proposed revisions did not address Powell's concerns:

> I do not believe that the discussion of the manner in which the prosecutor actually exercised his peremptory challenges can be completely ignored. I think it necessary to point out that harmless error analysis cannot be applied in this case because the exclusion of Bounds cannot be seen as an isolated incident when in reality others were excluded on the same basis by use of peremptory challenges. Inasmuch as you remain concerned about this discussion, I have renumbered it as a separate section. Thus, if you are at all disposed to join the rest—or any part—of the opinion, you can do so without that section. (Blackmun 1987l)

After this letter, Powell decided to join all but that part of Blackmun's opinion. According to a memo from Blackmun's clerk, "[t]he gist of the [concurrence] is going to be that he adheres to *Davis* and that how the prosecutor uses his peremptory challenges is irrelevant" (Blackmun 1987m).

Although Blackmun needed Powell as a fifth vote, he still refused to completely accommodate Powell's concerns. He attempted to accommodate as much as he could, but he ultimately chose to address the issue of how the prosecutor used his peremptory challenges. This issue was important to Blackmun, so important that he insisted even though he knew he was losing Powell's vote for the opinion. He did, however, restructure the opinion in such a way that Powell could join the rest of the opinion instead of only joining the judgment.

Similarly, in *Gwaltney v. Chesapeake Bay Foundation* (1987), which involved whether Section 505(a) of the Clean Water Act confers federal jurisdiction over citizen suits for wholly past violations, Marshall refused to fully accommodate concerns raised by some of the justices, which led to a concurrence. After circulating his draft, Stevens raised two concerns in a memo.

> First, I believe we should omit the words "for past violations of the Act" in lines 9 and 10 on page 8. It is clear that a citizen may recover civil penalties for violations of the Act that occur

> after the complaint is filed, but I am not at all sure that such a recovery for "past violations"—i.e., those that occurred before the suit was filed—are authorized by [Section] 505. In any event, I do not think it is necessary implicitly to decide this point in this case. Second, I'm not sure it is necessary to decide whether a mere allegation of continuous or intermittent violation is sufficient to confer jurisdiction or, in the alternative, whether there must be some such proof to support jurisdiction. (Marshall 1987g)

That same day, Scalia wrote Marshall, letting him know that he was circulating a separate concurrence on the point discussed in Part III of the opinion—whether a good faith allegation is all that is required for jurisdiction under Section 505. He then stated: "I would like to join the remainder of the opinion, but it resolves, or appears to suggest resolution, of one issue that I thought we had agreed to leave unanswered, and another that was not discussed. I hope you may be able to accept some changes on these points." He then suggested a change to the opinion. "This leaves it unresolved whether the past violation must be the same as the ongoing violation, whereas the present formulation seemingly envisions that one ongoing violation can support penalties for multiple past ones." Scalia also wrote that the opinion suggests that the plaintiff does not have to offer proof of his allegations of standing in response to a motion for summary judgment, which, according to him, is inconsistent with *Celotex Corp. v. Catrett* (1986). "I hope that the opinion can be amended to reflect the holding of *Celotex*" (Marshall 1987h).

O'Connor then sent Marshall a memo, in which she stated: "I share Nino's and John's concerns about the jurisdictional issue in Part III and about the problem of recovery for past violations joined with an ongoing violation. For now, I will wait to see what changes you make in the circulating draft" (Marshall 1987i). Marshall responded to the concerns raised by Scalia and Stevens, and agreed to delete the phrase that Stevens suggested. However, he refused to ignore the good faith allegation question and also wrote: "On the merits of the good faith allegation issue, I stand by my opinion." He then wrote: "As for Nino's *Celotex* point, I fail to see that the *Gwaltney* opinion says anything inconsistent with *Celotex*. . . . My statement of the summary judgment standard in *Gwaltney* . . . in no way suggests that the nonmoving party may prevail upon a complete failure of proof concerning an essential element of that party's case" (Marshall 1987j).

Scalia then responded, stating that Marshall's agreement with Steven's suggestion fully met his concern. He then wrote: "On the *Celotex* point, I am glad to know that we have no disagreement." He then asked Marshall to revise the three sentences in question to reflect their agreement. Finally, Scalia addressed the good faith allegation issue. He stated that he agreed it would be preferable to address the issue, although he could join if Marshall would take the suggestion proposed by Stevens.

> On the merits, I agree that it is inconceivable how it could make any difference in these Clean Water Act cases. But that only makes me all the more reluctant to acknowledge that Congress has so subtly created such an unusual jurisdictional provision—which will become known as "Gwaltney-type jurisdiction," and may be discovered in other statutes where it will make a difference. For our benefit, as well as the benefit of the legislators who vote upon bills, it seems to me an important part of sound judicial practice not to discern such an irregular disposition where it has not been clearly created. (Marshall 1987k)

Marshall responded to Scalia's memo, proposing a modification in response to his *Celotex* concerns. "I think that this change makes clear our common understanding that the nonmoving party cannot prevail without introducing evidence from which the trial judge could conclude that there remains a genuine issue of material fact regarding the truth of the allegations of standing." However, on the good faith allegation issue, Marshall was not persuaded by Scalia's argument. "I believe my reading of Congress' intent accords with the plain language of [Section] 505 and with a logical and reasonable congressional intent. Moreover, I continue to conclude that our difference on this matter is of no practical consequence for this or any other statute." He ended the memo by stating: "In sum, I am inclined to keep Part III of my circulating opinion as it now stands, except for the modification proposed" (Marshall 1987l).

Stevens wrote another memo to Marshall, thanking him for his response. He then wrote:

> I remain troubled by one fact, but it is somewhat different from Nino's concern. It is this: The statute says nothing about "good faith," and I do not believe that the subjective good faith of the plaintiff or the plaintiff's attorney can have any impact on the district court's jurisdiction to determine whether there really is an ongoing violation of the statute. In my opinion an allegation of such a violation must give the district court jurisdiction to determine whether the defendant is in fact engaged in a continuous or intermittent violation (or perhaps threatens to do so), but if the allegation cannot be proved, I think it is clear that the district court must dismiss the complaint. Whether it is a dismissal on the merits or for want of jurisdiction is not a matter of any

importance. I am, however, concerned about the introduction of a new, non-statutory "good faith" test of jurisdiction.

Stevens then asked Marshall to make four "rather minor changes," stating that "[i]f you can make these changes or something similar, I will be happy to join your opinion" (Marshall 1987m).

The next day, Scalia, responding to Marshall, thanked him for the proposed changes addressing his *Celotex* concern. He then acknowledged that they remained in disagreement on the good-faith allegation point; however, he stated that he "would not feel it necessary to write separately if the proposals contained in John's ... memo were adopted" (Marshall 1987n).

Although Marshall could have accommodated Stevens' suggested changes and prevented a concurrence, he chose not to.

> Those changes, although not extensive, would sidestep the issue of the sufficiency of good faith allegations to support subject-matter jurisdiction under [Section] 505(a), a matter ruled on by the District Court and commented upon by the Circuit Court.... I believe that we owe the lower courts and the parties in this case a ruling on this issue. For that reason, I am inclined to keep Part III as it stands. (Marshall 1987o)

Marshall received the following response from Stevens: "Thanks for considering my suggestions. Since I think I am a little closer to Nino's position than yours with regard to Part III, I am joining his separate writing; that also means that I am joining your Parts I and II" (Marshall 1987p). Thus, it appears that since it was important to Marshall to address the issue by clarifying the law for the lower courts, he did not accommodate the justices and the result was a concurrence.

Griffith v. Kentucky (1987) provides another example of an unsuccessful negotiation that led to a concurrence. In *Griffith*, the issue was whether a newly declared constitutional rule was applicable to litigation pending on direct state or federal review or not yet final when the rule was decided. The newly declared constitutional rule at issue came from *Batson*, where the Court ruled that a defendant in a state criminal trial could establish a prima facie case of racial discrimination based on the prosecution's use of peremptory challenges to strike members of the defendant's race from the jury venire, and that, once the defendant had made the prima facie showing, the burden shifted to the prosecution to come forward with a neutral explanation for those challenges.

Regarding retroactivity, Justice John Marshall Harlan II had expressed his view in his concurrence in the judgment in *Mackey v. United States* (1971).

> If we do not resolve all cases before us on direct review in light of our best understanding of governing constitutional principles, it is difficult to see why we should so adjudicate any case at all. . . . In truth, the Court's assertion of power to disregard current law in adjudicating cases before us that have not already run the full course of appellate review, is quite simply an assertion that our constitutional function is not one of adjudication but in effect of legislation. (*Mackey* 1971, 679)

In *United States v. Johnson* (1982), the Court's acceptance of Justice Harlan's views led them to hold that a decision of the Court construing the Fourth Amendment was to be applied retroactively to all convictions that were not yet final at the time the decision was rendered. However, there were exceptions, one of which was the "clear break" exception. Under this exception, a new constitutional rule was not to be applied retroactively, even to cases on direct review, if the new rule explicitly overruled a past precedent of the Court, disapproved a practice the Court had sanctioned in prior cases, or overturned a longstanding practice that lower courts had uniformly approved.

Before the draft of the opinion, Blackmun's clerk spoke with Powell's clerk about the case. "Apparently, Justice Powell feels very strongly that Batson should be applied retroactively to cases on direct appeal, following his oft-repeated view that Justice Harlan's approach should be accepted. (I.e., Justice Powell does not believe that the 'clear break' exception set out in Johnson for cases on direct appeal should exist.)" (Blackmun 1986g).

Blackmun received a memo from Stevens, asking him to make two changes in the text and omit two footnotes. If he made those changes, Stevens would join the opinion. "You have properly confined the scope of your opinion to the problem presented by cases on direct appeal. My concerns are that the two footnotes and text passages might come back to haunt us when we are squarely confronted with the question whether to adopt Justice Harlan's analysis on collateral review cases"[25] (Blackmun 1986h). Blackmun then received a memo from Scalia: "While I would prefer the opinion to suggest, however subtly, that we are adopting the entirety of Justice Harlan's analysis in *Mackey*, it is at least a condition of my joinder that it not imply a refusal to adopt the entirety of that analysis. The suggestions circulated by John would satisfy that concern, and I will join if they are adopted" (Blackmun 1986i). Blackmun then received a memo from Powell, recognizing that the opinion could be written narrowly, however stating his preference that Harlan's view be adopted in its entirety. He agreed with the views expressed by Stevens and Scalia, "and subject to your accepting John's suggestions, I will join your opinion." He then added: "Since I became a full convert to John Harlan's view in my concurring opinion in *Hankerson v. North Carolina*, I probably will write a brief concurring opinion" (Blackmun 1986j). Blackmun did not respond to this memo. Thus, at this point, there were three justices who wanted the same change.

Blackmun wrote a memo in which he enclosed a second draft of the majority opinion, which incorporated the changes Stevens suggested. Because the majority opinion was written more narrowly than he wanted, Powell wrote a regular concurrence. However, this concurrence was an expansive concurrence, which did not undercut the reasoning and rationale of the majority opinion, which perhaps explains why Blackmun did not seem overly concerned about Powell's concurrence.

Michigan v. Chesternut (1988) provides another example of a case in which negotiations failed. In this case, the officers' pursuit of the respondent did not constitute a "seizure" implicating the Fourth Amendment. First, Blackmun's clerk gave some insight into how this particular majority opinion was originally drafted.

> In writing this opinion, I felt I had two choices: I could write it broadly, stating in no uncertain terms that police conduct need not result in the actual detention of a suspect to constitute a seizure warranting protection under the Fourth Amendment, or I could write it narrowly, concluding simply that no seizure occurred in this case, and leave the question whether (and in what circumstances) a pursuit that did not result in detention could ever be characterized as a seizure for another day. As I mentioned to you a few days back, I decided that it was most prudent to take the latter, narrow approach. I have therefore drafted an opinion that is simple and brief. I'm concerned about avoiding a splintering of the Court over the broader question, and the facts of this case certainly don't require the Court to settle the question here.

In addition, the clerk stated the following:

> At Conference, Justice Scalia ranted and raved about the Court's failure to reach the second question: whether, if the pursuit constituted a Terry-stop type seizure, respondent's apparent attempt to flee from the police established the particularized suspicion required to justify that seizure. Justice Scalia points out that it was this second question that the Court was primarily concerned about in granting cert. That may well be, but I think the Court was right to decide that this case is the wrong case in which to try to reach the question. The determination whether the pursuit was a seizure at all appears to be a logical antecedent to an assessment

of the justification for any seizure that did occur. Nevertheless, Justice Scalia made some noises about writing separately to reach this second question. (I gather he would assume the existence of a seizure and proceed directly to this second question). I spoke with his clerk recently to learn whether Justice Scalia was still planning to write. His clerk hopes he will drop the idea, but wasn't overly optimistic, given the virulence of his initial reaction. Another reason, I think, for you [not] to write a dramatic, splashy opinion in this case. (Blackmun 1988h)

The draft of the opinion that was circulated ended up stating: "Rather than adopting either rule proposed by the parties and determining that an investigatory pursuit is or is not necessarily a seizure under the Fourth Amendment, we adhere to our traditional contextual approach, and determine only that, in this particular case, the police conduct in question did not amount to a seizure." According to the clerk, although the opinion did not preclude the Court from finding in subsequent cases that certain pursuits with a manifest intent to capture constitute seizures, it in no way commanded a finding of a seizure under any given circumstances. It left for "another day the determination of the circumstances in which police pursuit could amount to a seizure under the Fourth Amendment."

Scalia wrote a memo to Blackmun, in which he argued that the opinion was not as narrow as he had hoped "because it decides the issue whether the fact that a person is fleeing prevents the conclusion that he has been seized." He added:

> I had thought what the opinion would say was that, whether or not continuing flight might prevent a seizure, and whether or not evidence acquired as the result of an attempted unconstitutional seizure comes within the exclusionary rule, there is no seizure when the facts give rise to no reasonable belief on the part of the defendant that his liberty was sought to be restrained.

He suggested an alteration to the opinion because he preferred not to write separately (Blackmun 1988i).

Kennedy also expressed concern over the language of the opinion. "It seems to me that it in effect holds that if there is a pursuit, with an intent to apprehend, there is necessarily a seizure. I question that that should be the rule and, in any event, believe that the issue is not presented in this case." He ended by stating that he was "giving the matter further study" (Blackmun 1988j).

Blackmun's clerk responded: "Just to give you a little balance, Justice Stevens' clerk asked me to convey to you Justice Stevens' satisfaction (before receiving either Justice Kennedy or Justice Scalia's memos) with the fact that the opinion was so 'narrowly crafted.' Seems there's no pleasing everyone" (Blackmun 1988k).

Rehnquist also wrote a memo to Blackmun, sharing Scalia's concern that the opinion decided that flight alone would not preclude a finding that a seizure took place. "I see no reason to address this question, since all agree that respondent could not reasonably have concluded that he had been detained." He concluded with: "I will wait to see what you, Nino, and Tony work out before I take further action" (Blackmun 1988l).

According to Blackmun's clerk, "In a [Chester]nutshell, my current view is: 'We have six votes, so there'" (Blackmun 1988m). Blackmun then responded to Rehnquist, Scalia, and Kennedy, starting off by telling the justices he had six votes for the opinion as originally circulated. He then agreed to some of the other changes they suggested, but then explained why the opinion had been crafted the way it had. "The opinion in no way commands a finding of a seizure under any circumstances" (Blackmun 1988n). Scalia, joined by Kennedy, ended up writing the following concurrence:

> It is no bold step to conclude, as the Court does, that the evidence should have been admitted, for respondent's unprovoked flight gave the police ample cause to stop him. The Court instead concentrates on the significance of the chase; and as to that it is fair to interpret its opinion as finding no more than an absence of improper conduct. We would do well to add that, barring the need to inquire about hot pursuit, which is not at issue here, neither "chase" nor "investigative pursuit" need be included in the lexicon of the Fourth Amendment. A Fourth Amendment seizure occurs when an individual remains in the control of law enforcement officials because he reasonably believes, on the basis of their conduct toward him, that he is not free to go. See, e.g., INS v. Delgado, 466 U.S. 210, 215 United States v. Mendenhall, 446 U.S. 544, 554 (1980) (opinion of Stewart, J.). The case before us presented an opportunity to consider whether even an unmistakable show of authority can result in the seizure of a person who attempts to elude apprehension and who discloses contraband or other incriminating evidence before he is ultimately detained. It is at least plausible to say that whether or not the officers' conduct communicates to a person a reasonable belief that they intend to apprehend him, such conduct does not implicate

Fourth Amendment protections until it achieves a restraining effect. The Court's opinion does not foreclose this holding, and I concur. (*Chesternut* 1988, 578)

In this case, Blackmun did not have much incentive to accommodate Scalia and Kennedy since he already had six votes for his opinion. "Once majority acquiescence has been obtained, the marginal value of any additional vote declines perceptibly, as would the price which an opinion writer should be willing to pay" (Murphy 1964, 65).

Conclusion

By examining the memoranda between Blackmun and Marshall and the other justices and the memoranda from their clerks, this chapter provides insight into the bargaining and accommodation that occurred between Blackmun and Marshall and the other justices. Blackmun and Marshall accommodated their colleagues even when suggestions were not contingent on joining, which suggests that cooperating is important to the justices. They also were more likely to accommodate when more than one justice wanted a particular change. However, neither justice accommodated suggestions when the issue was important to them and a majority of the justices had joined the opinion.

The memos also provide evidence that Blackmun and Marshall not only took into account how any accommodation would affect the substance of the opinion and their preferences about the particular issue involved, but they also took into account the other justices who had already joined the opinion. For example, Blackmun's colleagues, even those who were in ideological agreement, sometimes pulled Blackmun in two different directions. However, even when a justice was not satisfactorily accommodated, he or she would not necessarily write separately. This suggests that the justices, when considering their options, take into account the impact the opinion will have on the legal community.

The opinion writing process is complex and, although policy objectives clearly affect the justices' behavior, there are other factors that come into play. The justices have to take into account their colleagues on the bench, sometimes agreeing to join an opinion even when their most favored outcome is not achieved. However, there are times when the justices, although agreeing with the result of the decision, are not satisfactorily accommodated and they choose to write or join a concurrence. Does that choice to communicate publicly have an impact? I consider this question in the next chapter.

4

The Impact of Concurring Opinions

In *Katz v. United States* (1967), the Supreme Court considered the constitutionality of law enforcement officers placing a wiretap in a telephone booth without a search warrant. Katz was making a phone call in a public phone booth to allegedly engage in an illegal wagering transaction. Suspecting foul play, FBI agents placed an electronic recording device on the outside of the booth to record the defendant's conversation. The trial court admitted evidence of the conversations over Katz's objection. When Katz appealed, the Ninth Circuit Court of Appeals rejected his contention that the recordings of his telephone conversations violated the Fourth Amendment, relying on a previous case in which the Court held that the Fourth Amendment only applies to "places" and "things" and that the Amendment could only be violated by physical trespass onto the subject's property.

The Supreme Court, however, reversed the lower court and held that even though the agents did not physically trespass into a traditionally protected area, the agents were "searching" for purposes of the Fourth Amendment and had obtained information illegally without first securing a search warrant. "[W]hat [a person] seeks to preserve as private, even in an area accessible to the public, may be constitutionally protected" (351). The Court held that, in the absence of a judicially authorized search warrant, the wiretaps of the public phone booth used by Katz were illegal and, consequently, the evidence gathered against him from his conversations should be suppressed.

Although the majority took a radical new approach to the Fourth Amendment "search" issue, it is the language found in Justice John Marshall Harlan II's concurring opinion that emerged as the foundation for the *Katz* formula as it exists today.[1] Harlan agreed with the majority opinion of the Court, but he wrote to clarify when a person is entitled to Fourth Amendment protection. Expanding on the general principles enunciated by the majority opinion, Harlan proposed the following two-pronged test: "My understanding of the rule that has emerged from prior judicial decisions is that there is a twofold requirement, first that a person have exhibited an actual (subjective) expectation of privacy; and second, that the expectation be one that society is prepared to recognize as 'reasonable'" (361). This language became the core language in Fourth Amendment "search" jurisprudence, and both the Supreme Court and the lower federal courts have looked to this two-pronged test, and not the majority opinion, to determine when a person is entitled to Fourth Amendment protection. Thus, it is the concurrence that has come to be seen as the main point of the *Katz* decision.

Katz demonstrates the potential impact that concurrences can have, yet the question remains whether a systematic impact exists. As discussed in Chapter 1, concurrences are theoretically puzzling because the justice who writes or joins a concurrence agrees with the result reached by the Court, yet seeks to limit, expand, clarify, or change the grounds for the opinion. What impact do these concurring opinions have?

Some scholars argue that concurrences have a negative effect because a decision accompanied by a concurrence speaks with less authority (see Ray 1990). Moreover, concurring opinions are inconsistent with traditional consensus norms (Walker, et al. 1988) and they represent "modes of conflict on the Supreme Court" (Caldeira and Zorn 1998, 877). The argument is that the majority opinion is weakened by the presence of concurring opinions (see, e.g., Hansford and Spriggs 2006; Spriggs and Hansford 2001) and, consequently, the Supreme Court and the lower courts will be more likely to treat a precedent accompanied by a concurrence negatively. Hansford and Spriggs (2006) investigated whether lower federal courts respond to how the Supreme Court has interpreted one of its precedents. As a control variable, they included the number of special concurrences that accompanied a precedent. Their results indicated that this variable did not reveal any systematic influence on the lower courts' treatment of precedent. In contrast, Spriggs and Hansford (2001) examined why and when the Supreme Court chooses to overrule one of its own precedents and found that the larger the number of concurring opinions that were published with a precedent, the greater the chance it will be overruled. However, no one has examined the content of concurrences in an effort to explain whether the *type* of concurrence influences lower court compliance and subsequent treatment by the Supreme Court. As shown earlier, some concurrences support the majority opinion and others do not. For example, a concurring opinion may clarify the outcome of the case and strengthen the result. However, a concurrence can also detract from the impact of the majority opinion by disagreeing with the reasoning of the majority and pointing out the flaws of the opinion. Thus, differentiating between the types of concurrences can illuminate the true impact they have.

Specifically, I test whether different types of concurrences have differential effects on the U.S. Courts of Appeals and the Supreme Court. I find that concurrences that signal stronger support for majority opinions increase the extent to which the Circuit Courts positively interpret the

Supreme Court majority opinion, whereas concurrences that strongly disagree with the majority opinion decrease the extent to which the Circuit Courts positively interpret the majority opinion. This research is important because it addresses the ability of the Supreme Court to act as a final arbiter of federal law. If a justice writes a concurrence that disagrees with the reasoning of the majority and the Circuit Court finds the concurrence persuasive and chooses to rely on that concurrence, the precedent handed down by the majority is weakened. Additionally, this research increases our understanding of both Supreme Court and Circuit Court decision making. The justices send signals to the lower courts through concurrences and the lower courts are using these signals.

Similarly, I find that a precedent accompanied by an expansive concurrence increases the likelihood that the Supreme Court will positively treat the precedent, whereas a precedent accompanied by a doctrinal concurrence decreases the likelihood that the Supreme Court will positively treat the precedent. This indicates that the Supreme Court and the Circuit Courts of Appeals are reacting to the types of concurrences in a similar way.

The Impact of Concurring Opinions on Lower Court Compliance

Concurrences and Lower Court Compliance

Although scholarship has provided empirical support for the proposition that the lower federal courts generally follow precedents established by the Supreme Court (see Benesh 2002; Gruhl 1980; Songer and Sheehan 1990), shirking (or noncompliance) still occurs. Scholars have been interested in whether lower courts follow the Supreme Court's rulings or "shirk" by taking positions not compatible with the Court's doctrine. Scholars have defined compliance as following the legal rules or doctrine adopted by the Court (see, e.g., Benesh 2002).Individuals and organizations are guided by the Court's legal rules, which constitute "the core of the Court's policy-making process" (Wahlbeck 1997, 780). These principles embodied in the Court's opinions create precedent to guide the decisions of the lower courts. Lower courts that disagree with the higher court may evade their mandates (Canon 1973). They can interpret a Supreme Court decision very narrowly, basically limiting it to its specific facts (Canon and Johnson 1999). They may distinguish their case from the Supreme Court case (Caminker 1994; Baum 1978; Songer and Sheehan 1990). They even may question or criticize the case (Tarr 1977). If the lower courts do not follow the legal rules or doctrine announced by the Supreme Court, the impact of that decision is diminished and, consequently, the impact of the Supreme Court is diminished.

What factors, then, affect whether the Supreme Court obtains full compliance from the lower federal courts? Studies have shown that there are a number of legal and attitudinal variables that influence the level of compliance by the lower courts, such as the age, complexity, and importance of the precedent, ideological consistency between the lower court and the Supreme Court precedent, the current ideology of the Supreme Court, and whether the precedent has been overruled (see, e.g., Benesh and Reddick 2002; Brenner and Spaeth 1995; Brent 1999; Gruhl 1980; Johnson 1987; Klein 2002; Wasby 1970).

Another factor is how authoritative a Supreme Court case appears to a lower court judge. Lower courts may be more likely to follow the Supreme Court decision if they perceive the Court is strongly united in its decision. Scholars have used different measures to capture the authoritativeness of a Supreme Court decision, including whether it was unanimous, whether it was a minimum winning coalition decision, the size of the voting majority, the number of dissenting justices, the number of dissenting opinions, and the number of special concurring opinions (Benesh and Reddick 2002; Hansford and Spriggs 2006; Johnson 1979).

As stated previously, the assumption is that concurring opinions decrease compliance by lower courts. Specifically, the mere presence of a concurring opinion may transform a majority opinion into a plurality. A plurality opinion is one in which a majority of the Court agrees to the result, but less than a majority of the justices agree to the reasons behind the decision. The plurality opinion generally is regarded as a source of uncertainty and instability in the law, creating confusion in lower courts that are bound to follow the precedent established by the Supreme Court. A recent study confirms that lower courts are less likely to comply with plurality decisions than majority decisions (Corley 2009).

Moreover, concurring opinions may undermine the force of a unanimous Court. The Court recognized the importance of a unified response to a case of major significance, as illustrated by *Brown v. Board of Education* (1954). In deciding *Brown* and the companion school segregation cases, Chief Justice Warren wished to avoid concurring opinions. "He wanted a single, unequivocating opinion that could leave no doubt that the Court had put Jim Crow to the sword" (Kluger 1977, 683). Warren recalled in his memoirs:

> To have affirmed these cases without decision and with the mere statement that it was being done by an equally divided Court, if such had been the case, would have aborted the judicial process and resulted in public frustration and disrespect for the Court. The Court was thoroughly conscious of the importance of the decision to be arrived at and the impact it would have on the

nation. With this went realization ... for achieving unity, if possible. (Warren 1977, 282)

Beyond the mere presence of a concurring opinion, however, the content of the concurrences is important to understand. The justice agrees with the result, yet seeks to limit, expand, clarify, or change the grounds for an otherwise authoritative majority opinion. In fact, concurrences advance the dialogue of the law, with the justices using concurrences to provide cues and signals to each other, the legal community, and Congress. "[T]he system of separate opinions has made the Supreme Court the central forum of current legal debate, and has transformed its reports from a mere record of reasoned judgment into something of a History of American Legal Philosophy with Commentary" (Scalia 1994, 40). Thus, concurrences highlight the difference between voting for the *result* and voting for the *opinion*. One scholar argues:

> [J]ustices care most about the underlying legal principles in an opinion, rather than just which side wins the case. The justices want legal policy to reflect their policy preference because they understand that it is those policies that ultimately influence distributional consequences in society. It is the legal rule announced in an opinion (not which party won the case) that ultimately serves as referents for behavior and alters the perceived costs and benefits decision makers attach to alternative courses of action. (Spriggs 2003)

How can concurrences affect compliance by the lower courts? A concurrence may be more revealing than a justice's majority opinion because it is not the product of compromise (see Wahlbeck, et al. 1999). "To be able to write an opinion solely for oneself, without the need to accommodate, to any degree whatever, the more-or-less differing views of one's colleagues; to address precisely the points of law that one considers important and no others ... that is indeed an unparalleled pleasure" (Scalia 1994, 42). Thus, the concurrence can signal to the lower courts how a particular justice views a given issue and how that justice may be expected to vote in the future. Studies have shown that lower courts engage in anticipatory compliance, seeking to interpret a Supreme Court precedent according to how the current Supreme Court would interpret that precedent and concurrences provide information that the lower courts can use to interpret the precedent accordingly. For example, in *Coy v. Iowa* (1988), the defendant was charged with sexually assaulting two thirteen-year-old girls. The girls were permitted to testify with a screen placed between them and the defendant. The Court reversed Coy's conviction on the grounds that the procedure violated the defendant's right to confrontation. However, the Court acknowledged that the rights preserved in the Confrontation Clause are not absolute and conceded that exceptions might be justified "when necessary to further an important public policy" (1021). Justice O'Connor wrote a concurring opinion, stating that confrontation rights "are not absolute but rather may give way in an appropriate case to other competing interests so as to permit the use of certain procedural devices designed to shield a child witness from the trauma of courtroom testimony" (1022). This statement was prophetic of her reasoning in the majority opinion of *Maryland v. Craig* (1990), where the Court held that a defendant's right to confrontation was not violated by permitting a six-year-old child to testify at trial via one-way closed-circuit television in a case of sexual abuse. The Court reasoned that Maryland had an important interest in preserving the physical and psychological well-being of the child witness.

Connected to this idea of the lower courts engaging in anticipatory compliance is the fact that the concurrence may signal how much support the opinion has. However, it is not the mere presence of a concurrence, but what the concurrence says that is important. Reagan administration lawyers wrote that Justice O'Connor had a "troublesome propensity to file concurring opinions seeking to dilute the force of opinions condemning racial quotas" (Greenburg 2007, 44). Thus, the concurring opinion may signal that the concurring opinion writer does not fully support all aspects of the reasoning of the opinion, highlighting how the majority opinion should be limited, or even how it can be distinguished in future cases. One study demonstrated that justices who author or join special concurring opinions (specifically disagreeing with the majority's rationale) in precedent-setting cases are more likely to overrule these precedents than members of the majority coalition who do not author or join such concurring opinions (Collins 2004). The concurring opinion may, however, signal that the concurring opinion writer believes the opinion did not go far enough and the justice is willing to apply the reasoning to a multitude of factual situations. Moreover, the concurrence may supplement the reasoning, giving additional, persuasive arguments for reaching that result.

Additionally, a concurrence can provide cues to the lower courts about how to interpret the Constitution by giving guidance on how to interpret the Court's majority opinion. Baum (1978) suggests that the impact of the Supreme Court should increase as the clarity of its opinions increase. A concurring opinion may provide much needed clarification that increases the ability of the lower court to understand and accept the opinion.

Finally, the concurrence may directly confront the arguments made in the majority opinion, pointing out weaknesses or flaws in the reasoning of the majority. Concurring and majority opinions "compete with each other to win over future judges and scholars" (Kolsky 1995, 2085). Thus, lower court judges may find themselves persuaded by the reasoning of the concurring opinion when interpreting the Supreme Court majority opinion.

Specifying a Model of the Impact of Concurring Opinions on Lower Court Compliance

As discussed in Chapter 1, concurrences can be categorized into six different types. The first category, the *expansive concurrence*, attempts to expand the holding or to supplement the reasoning of the majority opinion. Because this type of concurrence gives a lower court judge more reason to extend the Supreme Court's reasoning to their specific case, my first hypothesis is as follows:

> A lower court is more likely to comply with a Supreme Court decision that is accompanied by an expansive concurrence.

The second category is the *doctrinal concurrence*, which is a concurrence that offers a different theory to support the Court's result. This is the "right result, wrong reason" concurrence (Ray 1990, 800). This concurrence generally rejects the entire foundation of the Court's opinion, concurring in the judgment but for an entirely different reason. Thus, these concurrences disagree with the majority opinion, even though the opinion writer agrees with the final outcome of the case (who wins and who loses). Because a doctrinal concurrence disagrees with the reasoning used by the majority opinion, and does not support the rules or doctrine adopted by the Court, my second hypothesis is:

> A lower court is less likely to comply with a Supreme Court decision that is accompanied by a doctrinal concurrence.

The third category is the *limiting concurrence*, a concurring opinion that attempts to limit or qualify the holding. The opinion writer argues that certain parts of the majority's discussion were unnecessary or thinks the Court has gone too far in its reasoning or conclusions. The "concurrer acts to rein in the doctrinal force of the majority" (Ray 1990, 784). The concurrence may limit the majority opinion to the particular circumstances of the case under review or may "take the majority to task for addressing an issue not properly before it" (Ray 1990, 785).

The tendency for these limiting concurrences is towards contraction. Moreover, a limiting concurrence can signal to the lower court that support for the majority decision is not high, and provide a rationale for the lower court to not comply with the case. Thus, my third hypothesis is as follows:

> A lower court is less likely to comply with a Supreme Court case that has a limiting concurrence.

The fourth category is the *reluctant concurrence*. Here, the opinion writer makes it clear that he does not want to join the majority's decision, but feels compelled to, perhaps because of precedent or because of a desire to produce a majority opinion on an important issue. "This type of concurrence frequently originates in an earlier dissent" and "it resembles [a dissent] more than a concurrence" (Witkin 1977, 224). Thus, it weakens the authority of the majority opinion in much the same manner as a dissent and, consequently, I expect that

> A lower court is less likely to comply with a Supreme Court case that is accompanied by a reluctant concurrence.

The fifth category is the *emphatic concurrence*, which emphasizes some aspect of the Court's holding (see Ray 1990), and functions largely as a means of clarification. Because an emphatic concurrence agrees in full with the reasoning used by the majority and is merely emphasizing or highlighting some aspect of the opinion, and perhaps providing clarity that should lead to increased compliance (see Canon and Johnson 1999) I hypothesize the following:

> A lower court is more likely to comply with a Supreme Court case that is accompanied by an emphatic concurrence.

Finally, the last category is the *unnecessary concurrence*, which is a concurrence in judgment without opinion. Although this type of concurrence does not offer any justification or rationale for its disagreement and, consequently, may leave little impression on the lower court judges applying the decision, the concurrence does signal lack of support for the reasoning contained in the opinion. Thus, I hypothesize:

> A lower court is less likely to comply with a Supreme Court case accompanied by an unnecessary concurrence.

Although the focus is on concurring opinions and their effect on compliance, I also control for the following factors, which have been identified in past research as influencing lower court compliance:

1. *Dissents.* Given that dissents disagree with both the result of the majority decision and the reasoning, I expect that as the number of dissents that accompany a Supreme Court case increases, the less positively the lower court will treat the case.

2. *Age of Precedent.* There are two different views of how the age of a precedent might figure into the compliance decision. Either older decisions have become fundamental to the Court and lower courts would be more likely to follow those cases or recent precedents deserve more respect from the lower courts because the Supreme Court is not likely to overturn recently established precedents (see Brenner and Spaeth 1995). This variable is measured in years.

3. *Complexity.* The literature also provides competing hypotheses regarding lower court compliance with complex decisions. Wasby (1970) views complex decisions as confusing to the lower courts and thus expects them to limit compliance. On the other hand, Johnson (1987) found that complex decisions were followed more often and Benesh and Reddick (2002) viewed complex decisions as fostering higher levels of compliance because they engender a closer reading. For this variable, I rely on data from Spaeth (2007) and I count the number of legal provisions relied on and additional issues raised in the precedent (see Benesh and Reddick 2002).

4. *Ideological Incompatibility with Supreme Court Majority Opinion.* According to the literature (see, e.g., Hall and Brace 1992; Songer and Haire 1992), ideology does influence lower court judges, and as the distance between the ideology of the Supreme Court decision and the majority members of the deciding appeals court panel increases, the likelihood of the panel complying with the precedent should decrease. I use the Judicial Common Space score (Epstein, Martin, Segal and Westerland 2007) for each federal court of appeals judge, district court judge,[2] and each Supreme Court justice, a measure of personal ideology that places them in the same policy space. To generate a measure of the ideological distance between the majority members of the deciding appeals court panel in each case and the precedent, I take the absolute value of the difference between the median ideological score

of the majority members of the deciding appeals court panel and the ideological score of the majority opinion writer for the precedent case. This distance should capture whether the appeals court panel that treats the precedent is ideologically consistent with the Supreme Court decision.[3]

5. *Importance.* Although some scholars argue that important Supreme Court cases are more likely to be followed by lower courts because they are more visible (see Benesh and Reddick 2002), important cases are also more likely to be controversial, and a number of scholars (Baum 1978; Gruhl 1980; Wasby 1970) have suggested that noncompliance is most likely to occur in response to Supreme Court decisions that are controversial. I use two measures to tap into the importance of a Supreme Court case.[4] The first is a measure of *political importance*, a dichotomous variable coded 1 if the case is a major case using *The New York Times* measure and 0 otherwise (Epstein and Segal 2000).[5] The second is a measure of *legal importance*, also a dichotomous variable, coded 1 if the Supreme Court case according to Spaeth (2007) struck down a law as unconstitutional or overturned an existing precedent, and 0 otherwise.

6. *Change in Supreme Court Ideology.* The deciding appeals court panel may engage in anticipatory behavior, taking into consideration the ideology of the Supreme Court that is sitting at the time they interpret the precedent in an attempt to decide what the Supreme Court would do in the case. This may be because they fear reversal by the Supreme Court or because they believe that is their proper role. According to Klein (2002), two federal appellate judges indicated that they sometimes engage in anticipatory decision making. "That even two judges profess to decide some cases as they think the Supreme Court would is evidence that anticipatory decision-making occurs in the courts of appeals" (Klein 2002, 109). Additionally, Gruhl (1981) examined whether lower federal court judges anticipated new Supreme Court policy in the area of libel and found that "[l]ower federal court decisions to act in anticipatory compliance were the rule rather than the exception" (308). To measure this possibility, I use the change in Supreme Court ideology from the time of the precedent. I take the absolute value of the difference between the median ideological score of the Court sitting at the time the lower

court treats the decision from the median ideological score of the justices sitting at the time of the precedent.

7. *Treatment by the Supreme Court.* The U.S. Supreme Court can affect whether the lower court treats its precedent positively by how the Supreme Court treats its own precedent in subsequent cases. Hansford and Spriggs (2006) found that the more the Supreme Court has interpreted a precedent in a positive manner, the more frequently lower federal courts will follow the precedent. The more that the Court interprets a precedent negatively, the less often lower courts will follow the precedent. To measure this, I use *Shepard's Citations* to count the number of times the Court's majority opinions interpreted the precedent in a positive or negative manner before the lower court treats the precedent. The first variable, *positive Supreme Court treatment*, is the number of times the Court's majority opinions interpreted the precedent in a positive manner before the lower court treats the precedent. The second variable, *negative Supreme Court treatment*, is the number of times the Court's majority opinions interpreted the precedent in a negative manner before the lower court treats the precedent.

8. *Overruled.* Brent (1999) showed that lower courts are willing to act as the agents of both the Supreme Court and Congress. To control for Supreme Court cases which have been overruled or superseded by statute, I include a dummy variable, which is equal to 1 if the case has been overruled by the Supreme Court or superseded by statute, 0 otherwise.[6] I expect that these cases are less likely to be followed by the lower court. I also include fixed effects for each of the 12 circuits, with the First Circuit omitted for identifiability; these serve as controls for circuit-level factors not expressly incorporated in the model.

Estimating a Model of the Impact of Concurring Opinions on Lower Court Compliance

To determine whether the type of concurrence influences compliance by the lower courts, I identify and examine all treatments in the U.S. Courts of Appeals of the Supreme Court cases from the 1986 term.[7] The unit of analysis is the lower court decision that cited a Supreme Court opinion from the 1986 term. My analysis starts with circuit court cases from 1986 and ends in 2003. I identify cases for analysis through *Shepard's Citations* via Lexis. *Shepard's* is a legal resource that provides a list of all subsequently decided cases for each published state and federal court case. For each Supreme Court decision, *Shepard's* provides a list of all the subsequent cases (Supreme Court, Courts of Appeals, District Courts, and state courts) that cite the decision.[8]

Shepard's also offers an editorial analysis indicating how the subsequent decision (the "citing" case) legally interpreted the previous decision (the "cited" case). According to *Shepard's*, a cited case is not considered legally interpreted simply because the subsequent case cites it. Instead, it is necessary for the subsequent case to contain specific language that legally interprets the cited case (see Spriggs and Hansford 2000).[9] The goal of *Shepard's* is to ascertain whether the precedent is still good law, or whether it has been diminished in some way (Hansford and Spriggs 2006). Because I am interested in whether lower courts are complying, which involves "proper application of standards enunciated by the Supreme Court in deciding all cases raising similar or related questions," versus not complying, which "involves a failure to apply—or properly to apply—those standards" (Tarr 1977, 35), *Shepard's* is a valid indicator of compliance.

Shepard's offers for each citing case the following types of legal interpretations that are relevant to this study: questioned, limited, criticized, distinguished, followed, explained, or harmonized.[10] *Shepard's* labels followed as positive treatment and questioned, limited, criticized, and distinguished as negative treatment. Although *Shepard's* codes treatments of precedent that occur in concurring and dissenting opinions, I focus only on the treatments that occurred in majority opinions.

Shepard's uses followed to indicate that a citing case's majority opinion "expressly" relied on a cited case as precedent (Spriggs and Hansford 2000, 330). Examples of language that lead to an opinion being coded by *Shepard's* as followed are "controlling," or "determinative" or "such a conclusion is required by" (Spriggs and Hansford 2000, 330). This is a positive treatment and indicates full compliance by the lower court with the rule of law announced by the Supreme Court. Thus, I code a circuit case that *Shepard's* indicates followed a Supreme Court decision as positive.[11] Consistent with *Shepard's* typology of legal treatment, I code a case that questioned, limited, criticized, or distinguished a Supreme Court decision as negative, which indicates noncompliance with the Supreme Court case. The *Shepard's* coding scheme categorizes distinguished treatments as weaker negative treatments than treatments coded as criticized or limited. Nevertheless, when the lower court distinguishes a Supreme Court precedent, it explicitly chooses not to apply the precedent. In so doing, the lower court limits the impact of the Supreme Court decision to a narrower set of facts, and thus limits the potential impact on future cases, regardless of the motivation of the lower court or whether others would consider the treatment reasonable.[12] I exclude cases that explained or harmonized the precedent because those treatments are considered neutral.[13] The result of all these selection procedures and considerations is a sample of 2,747 lower federal court treatments.

Results

Table 4.1 presents the data used in the analysis.

Of 126 orally argued, signed Supreme Court opinions, 6 percent contained an expansive concurrence, 12 percent doctrinal, 14 percent limiting, 3 percent reluctant, 8 percent emphatic, 0.8 percent unnecessary, and 63 percent of the opinions did not contain a concurrence. From those 126 Supreme Court opinions, 2,747 lower federal court cases either positively or negatively interpreted those opinions. Eight percent of those cases were ones in which the Circuit Court was interpreting a Supreme Court case that contained an expansive concurrence, 10 percent doctrinal, 14 percent limiting, 1 percent reluctant, 6 percent emphatic, 0.2 percent unnecessary, and 68 percent of the Circuit Court cases were interpreting a Supreme Court case that did not contain a concurrence. Thus, the types of concurrences are distributed similarly between the Supreme Court cases and the Courts of Appeals cases interpreting those decisions.[14]

Given the dichotomous nature of the dependent variable, positive treatment, logistic regression analysis is employed. Table 4.2 (next page) summarizes the results. For interested readers, the full statistical results of the logit estimation appear in the appendix, along with descriptive statistics for all of the independent variables.

Table 4.1. Distribution of the Types of Concurrences: Supreme Court Versus Courts of Appeals

Type of Concurrence	Supreme Court	Courts of Appeals
Limiting	18 (14%)	383 (14%)
Doctrinal	15 (12%)	285 (10%)
Expansive	7 (6%)	207 (8%)
Emphatic	10 (8%)	165 (6%)
Reluctant	4 (3%)	31 (1%)
Unnecessary	1 (0.8%)	5 (0.2%)
None	79 (63%)	1,863 (68%)

Table 4.2. Summary of Model of Impact of Concurrences on Lower Court Compliance

Variable	Effect
Type of Concurrence	
Expansive	More likely
Doctrinal	Less likely
Limiting	No effect
Reluctant	No effect
Emphatic	No effect
Unnecessary	No effect
Control Variables	
Dissents	No effect
Age	More likely
Complexity	No effect
Ideological incompatibility	Less likely
Political importance	No effect
Legal importance	Less likely
Change in Supreme Court ideology	Less likely
Positive Supreme Court treatment	More likely
Negative Supreme Court treatment	Less likely
Overruled	Less likely

Effects of Concurrence Types

The results show that when concurrences were separated into different types, expansive and doctrinal concurrences influence lower court compliance.[15] As hypothesized, expansive concurrences have a positive impact and doctrinal concurrences have a negative impact.

Table 4.3 presents a variety of predicted probabilities associated with each of the statistically significant variables. The first row of the table shows the baseline probability of positive treatment by the lower federal courts. This baseline probability is computed by holding all variables at the mean or modal values and provides a useful starting point for evaluating the magnitude of the influence of each variable. Thus, the baseline probability is the probability of positive treatment when there are no concurrences accompanying the Supreme Court precedent.[16] As shown in Table 4.3, the likelihood of positive treatment is quite high at .762. The remaining rows in Table 4.3 report the predicted probabilities for each outcome as I set each statistically significant variable to different values, while holding all of the other variables constant at their respective baseline values.

As Table 4.3 shows, when the Supreme Court precedent contains no concurrences, the probability of positive treatment is .762. When the Supreme Court precedent contains an expansive concurrence, the probability of positive treatment by the lower court increases to .860. However, when the Supreme Court precedent contains a doctrinal concurrence, the probability of positive treatment by the lower court is reduced to .719.

Contrary to my hypotheses, limiting, emphatic, and unnecessary concurrences do not appear to influence lower court compliance. Perhaps this results from the fact that these concurrences are weaker forms of support or nonsupport for the majority decision. Doctrinal concurrences disagree entirely with the rationale used by the majority decision, whereas limiting concurrences do agree with the reasoning overall, but the opinion writer attempts to contract the reach of the decision. Expansive concurrences agree entirely with the rationale, and even signal that the opinion writer would even go further than the majority opinion went. Emphatic concurrences, on the other hand, do not add anything to the majority opinion, but simply reiterate some particular aspect of the opinion and unnecessary concurrences do not offer any reason why the justice is not joining the opinion coalition. Thus, it appears that the stronger concurrences (in terms of supporting or

Table 4.3. Predicted Probabilities of Positive Treatment by the Lower Courts

	Probability of Positive Treatment
Baseline	.762
Expansive concurrence	.860
Doctrinal concurrence	.719
Minimum age of Supreme Court precedent (0)	.713
Maximum age of Supreme Court precedent (17)	.821
Legally important Supreme Court precedent	.595
Minimum level of ideological compatibility (1.313)	.718
Maximum level of ideological compatibility (.0026)	.780
Minimum level of change in Supreme Court ideology (0)	.811
Maximum level of change in Supreme Court ideology (.563)	.644
Minimum number of positive treatments by Supreme Court (0)	.735
Maximum number of positive treatments by Supreme Court (5)	.900
Minimum number of negative treatments by Supreme Court (0)	.772
Maximum number of negative treatments by Supreme Court (3)	.644
Overruled Supreme Court precedent	.564

not supporting the majority opinions) influence the extent to which lower courts comply with the Supreme Court majority opinion.

Perhaps the only surprising result in Table 4.2 is the finding that reluctant concurrences have no impact on compliance by the lower court. The hypothesis that reluctant concurrences would weaken compliance behavior seemed well founded, but support for it is completely lacking. This may result from the fact that there are only four Supreme Court cases accompanied by a reluctant concurrence (and thirty-one lower court cases legally treating those cases).

Overall, these findings document that concurrences do influence lower court compliance. Doctrinal concurrences reduce compliance, providing the Courts of Appeals with wiggle room (Benesh 2002, 84). Just as a Supreme Court case may give lower courts wide latitude to carry out their policy, (see Canon and Johnson 1999), these types of concurrences provide lower court judges with more discretion by giving them a legitimate reason not to follow the precedent.[17] A doctrinal concurrence signals to the lower courts that there is disagreement with the reasoning employed by the majority opinion, perhaps pointing out weaknesses, detracting from the impact of the majority opinion. On the other hand, expansive concurrences increase lower court compliance by giving lower court judges more reason to extend the Supreme Court's reasoning to their specific case.

Control Variables

I now turn to a discussion of the results for the control variables. All but three of the control variables have a strong and statistically significant effect on lower court compliance. As I noted, scholars have disagreed about whether older or more recent Supreme Court cases are favored and whether case complexity has a positive or negative effect on whether Supreme Court precedents are likely to be followed by the lower courts. The results of this study show that both the age of the Supreme Court precedent and its complexity have positive impacts on lower court compliance. Specifically, when the Supreme Court decision is recent (less than one year old), the predicted probability of positive treatment is .713. When the Supreme Court decision is seventeen years old (the maximum age in the data), the predicted probability is .821. Additionally, legally important cases are less likely to be followed by the lower courts. The odds of positive treatment decrease by 16.7 percent when the Supreme Court case is legally important.

As predicted, as the distance between the ideology of the Supreme Court decision and the majority members of the deciding appeals court panel increases, the likelihood of the panel complying with the precedent decreases. When the ideology of the majority members of the deciding appeals court panel is ideologically consistent with the opinion, the predicted probability of positive treatment is .780, whereas when the ideology of the majority members of the deciding appeals court panel is not ideologically consistent with the opinion, the predicted probability of positive treatment decreases to .718.

As the current Supreme Court moves away from the precedent, the odds of the lower court positively treating the case decrease, consistent with Learned Hand's anticipatory theory: "I have always felt that it was the duty of an inferior court to suppress its own opinions and... try to prophesy what the appellate courts would do" (Baum 1978, 212). Specifically, when the ideology of the current Supreme Court is the same as the ideology of the Court that issued the precedent, the predicted probability of positive treatment is .811. When the ideology of the current Supreme Court and the Court that issued the precedent are far apart (maximum value of .563) the predicted probability of positive treatment drops to .644. Whether this provides evidence that lower court judges are engaging in strategic behavior, attempting to avoid reversal by the Supreme Court or whether the lower court judges are acting in accordance with how they view their role is not clear.

The number of positive and negative treatments the precedent has received by the Supreme Court also influences the likelihood of positive treatment by the Circuit Courts. As the number of positive treatments moves from the minimum level (zero) to the maximum level (five) the predicted probability of positive treatment increases by .165. As the number of negative treatments moves from the minimum level (zero) to the maximum level (three) the predicted probability of positive treatments decreases by .128.

Finally, cases that have been overruled by the Supreme Court or superseded by statute are less likely to be followed by the lower courts (56.4% vs. 76.2%). Thus, the lower courts are faithful to both principals—the Supreme Court and Congress.

Multiple Concurrences

During the 1986 term, twelve Supreme Court cases contained multiple concurrences, corresponding to 217 lower court decisions treating those cases. What happens when there are multiple concurrences? For instance, what if a Supreme Court case contains both an expansive and a doctrinal concurrence? In order to account for this, I ran a second regression, substituting a variable that captures how many concurrences support the Supreme Court majority opinion (expansive and emphatic) and how many concurrences do not support the majority opinion (doctrinal, limiting, and reluctant) for the types of concurrences in the first model. This variable, *net support*, is the difference between the number of supporting concurrences minus the number

Table 4.4. Summary of Model of Impact of Multiple Concurrences on Lower Court Compliance

Variable	Effect
Concurrences—Net Support	More likely
Control Variables	
Dissents	No effect
Age	More likely
Complexity	No effect
Ideological incompatibility	No effect
Political importance	No effect
Legal importance	Less likely
Change in Supreme Court ideology	Less likely
Positive Supreme Court treatment	More likely
Negative Supreme Court treatment	Less likely
Overruled	Less likely

of nonsupporting concurrences. I expect that as the number of supporting concurrences increases, the Circuit Courts will be more likely to positively interpret a Supreme Court precedent. I expect that as the number of nonsupporting concurrences increases, the Circuit Courts will be less likely to positively interpret a Supreme Court precedent.

Table 4.4 summarizes the estimation results. For interested readers, the full statistical results of the logit estimation appear in the appendix.

As Table 4.4 indicates, the more supportive concurrences that accompany the Supreme Court precedent, the more frequently lower federal courts will positively interpret the precedent. The more nonsupportive concurrences that accompany a Supreme Court precedent, the less likely it is that lower courts will positively interpret that precedent. Specifically, for each additional supportive concurrence, the odds of positive treatment by the circuit courts increases by 11.9 percent.

The Impact of Concurring Opinions on the Supreme Court's Interpretation of Its Own Precedent

The previous section examined the impact of concurrences on lower federal court compliance. Here, I examine the impact that concurrences have on the Supreme Court's interpretation of its own precedent. Just as different types of concurrences influence how lower court judges implement Court opinions, they may also affect how the justices react to their own opinions in the future (Spriggs and Hansford 2001).

Specifically, Spriggs and Hansford (2001) found that Supreme Court cases with a larger number of concurring opinions are more likely to be overruled in the future. Hansford and Spriggs (2006) found that the number of special concurring opinions accompanying the precedent increases the probability of negative interpretation by the Supreme Court but does not decrease the likelihood of the precedent being treated positively. The assumption is that "concurrences lower the credibility of a precedent and offer alternative legal rationales" (Spriggs and Hansford 2001, 1105) and that separate opinions "cause a precedent to be weaker" (Hansford and Spriggs 2006, 61). However, I propose that not all concurrences are the same; thus, it is theoretically reasonable to expect the Supreme Court's interpretation of its own precedent to be influenced by the type of concurrence that accompanies the precedent. More specifically, I test the following hypotheses regarding the Supreme Court's treatment of its own precedent:

> The Supreme Court is more likely to positively interpret a decision that is accompanied by an expansive or an emphatic concurrence.

> The Supreme Court is less likely to positively interpret a decision that is accompanied by a doctrinal, limiting, reluctant, or unnecessary concurrence.

Data and Methods

To test the effect of the different types of concurrences on the Supreme Court's interpretation of its own precedent, I examine how the Court interprets its own precedent from the 1986 term. Specifically, I identify and examine all treatments by the Supreme Court of cases from the 1986 term.[18] The unit of analysis is the Supreme Court decision that has cited a Court opinion from the 1986 term. My analysis starts with Supreme Court cases from 1986 and ends in 2003. As discussed earlier, I identify cases for analysis through *Shepard's Citations* via Lexis. Following *Shepard's*, I consider any Supreme Court decision that followed one of these precedents as treating the precedent positively. I code any decision in which the Supreme Court overruled, distinguished, limited, criticized, or questioned one of these precedents as negative treatment. I exclude cases that explained or harmonized the precedent because those treatments are considered neutral.[19] The result of all these selection procedures and considerations is a sample of 137 Supreme

Court cases.[20] The dependent variable is positive treatment, coded 1 if the Supreme Court positively interpreted the precedent, and 0 otherwise.

Independent Variables

The type of concurrence constitutes the independent variable of primary interest. As stated earlier, I coded the concurrences into six categories that I hypothesize should be useful in determining whether the *type* of concurrence influences how the Supreme Court interprets its own precedent. The categories are: expansive, doctrinal, limiting, reluctant, emphatic, and unnecessary (see Ray 1990; Witkin 1977). Each category was coded as one type of concurrence.

Although my primary focus is the effect of the different types of concurrences on the Supreme Court's interpretation of its precedent, I also control for alternative explanations. Therefore, I include the control variables used in the previous section: the number of dissents, age, complexity, importance of the precedent (whether the precedent is politically or legally important), the ideological compatibility between the precedent and the Court, whether the precedent has been overruled, and the net number of prior positive treatments by the Supreme Court.

Results

Table 4.5 summarizes the estimation results, indicating which variables did, in fact, manifest an influence and the direction of the substantive effect. This table shows the likelihood that the Supreme Court will positively treat the precedent. For interested readers, the full statistical results of the logit estimation appear in the appendix, along with descriptive statistics for all of the independent variables.

As Table 4.5 indicates, a precedent accompanied by an expansive concurrence increases the likelihood that the Supreme Court will positively treat the precedent while a precedent accompanied by a doctrinal concurrence decreases the likelihood that the Supreme Court will positively treat the precedent. This is consistent with the results obtained regarding lower court compliance with Supreme Court precedent, indicating that the Supreme Court and the Circuit Courts of Appeals are reacting to the types of concurrences in a similar way. An expansive concurrence signals that the majority opinion did not go far enough and that the justices writing or joining this type of concurrence would go farther in the future. On the other hand, a doctrinal concurrence signals less support for the majority opinion and its reasoning and the possibility that the Court will deal with the issue differently in the future. A decision accompanied by a doctrinal concurrence signals that the

Table 4.5. Summary of the Impact of the Type of Concurrence on the Supreme Court's Positive Treatment of Its Own Precedent

Variable	Effect
Type of Concurrence	
Expansive	Positive treatment *more* likely
Doctrinal	Positive treatment *less* likely
Limiting	No effect
Reluctant	No effect
Emphatic	No effect
Number of dissents	No effect
Age of precedent	No effect
Complexity	No effect
Political importance	No effect
Legal importance	Positive treatment *less* likely
Ideological incompatibility between Supreme Court and the precedent	Positive treatment *less* likely
Overruled	No effect
Prior positive net treatment by the Supreme Court	No effect

Court is not credibly committed to the legal rule and thus is less likely to follow that rule in the future.

Table 4.5 and the discussion so far has focused simply on which factors matter and whether they make positive treatment by the Supreme Court more or less likely. Based on the full estimation results (reported in the appendix), Table 4.6 presents a variety of predicted probabilities associated with each of the statistically significant variables in order to ascertain the meaning of the statistical results in substantive terms. The first row of the table shows the baseline predicted probability of positive treatment by the Supreme Court. This baseline probability is computed by holding all continuous variables (such as complexity) at their mean values, while holding all discrete variables (such as legally important) at their modal values. The resulting probabilities are the equivalent of the average probability of observing each outcome and provide a useful starting point for evaluating the magnitude of the influence of each variable.

As reported in Table 4.6 (next page), the baseline probability of positive treatment by the Supreme Court is .561. If the precedent contains an expansive concurrence, the probability of positive treatment increases to .960. On the other hand, if the precedent is accompanied by a doctrinal concurrence, the probability of positive treatment decreases to .215. Thus, the effects of these types of concurrences are quite substantial.

Table 4.6. Predicted Probabilities of Positive Treatment by the Supreme Court

	Probability of Positive Treatment
Baseline	.561
Expansive concurrence	.960
Doctrinal concurrence	.215
Legally important precedent	.140
Minimum level of ideological compatibility (5.114)	.405
Maximum level of ideological compatibility (.001)	.643

Turning to the control variables, only two influence whether the Supreme Court positively interprets past precedent. If a case is legally important, meaning that the case struck down a law as unconstitutional or overturned an existing precedent, then the Supreme Court is less likely to positively interpret the case. If the case is legally important, the probability that the Court will positively interpret the precedent decreases by .421. And the farther away the Supreme Court gets, ideologically speaking, from the precedent, the less likely the Court will positively interpret the precedent. For example, if the Court is not ideologically close to the precedent, the likelihood of positive treatment is .405. However, if the Court is ideologically close to the precedent, the likelihood of positive treatment is .643.

Conclusion

The Supreme Court, having neither purse nor sword, relies on the public and the other branches of government to turn law into action. The Court also must rely on lower federal courts to interpret and implement its decision. The evidence presented through my examination of the impact of concurrences indicates that concurrences do affect the extent to which lower courts positively interpret the Supreme Court majority opinion. When a justice writes or joins a concurrence, that justice sends a signal about the scope of the opinion, providing guidance to the lower courts about how to interpret the Court's opinion and apply it to factual situations in the future, and exhibiting the extent to which that justice agrees with the majority opinion. Similarly, the type of concurrence that accompanies the precedent influences the Supreme Court's interpretation of its own precedent. Specifically, I found that a precedent accompanied by an expansive concurrence increases the likelihood that the Supreme Court will positively treat the precedent, whereas a precedent accompanied by a doctrinal concurrence decreases the likelihood that the Supreme Court will positively treat the precedent. These findings support my general theoretical claim and show that court *opinions* matter, not just the vote on the merits, and specifically, that concurrences matter.

Although scholars have viewed concurrences as disagreement with the majority decision and there are concurrences that fit that description, some concurring opinions support the majority opinion. Thus, lumping concurrences into one category obscures the true impact that they have. The two strongest forms of concurrences, doctrinal and expansive, influence lower court compliance and the Supreme Court's subsequent treatment of precedent. In addition, the results show that the more supporting concurrences accompanying a Supreme Court precedent, the more likely the lower courts will positively interpret the decision. It remains to be seen whether the lower court judges are acting strategically, using the signals sent by concurrences to assess their risk of being reversed or as cover for minor acts of defiance or whether lower court judges are sincere actors who look to concurrences for information on what the law is. However, the implication is that lower court judges are receiving the signals being sent by the Supreme Court justices and these signals influence their behavior. Finally, these findings provide support for the argument that Supreme Court justices use concurrences to communicate their understanding and support of the majority decision to each other, and that this communication influences how the justices react to the precedent in the future.

5

Conclusion

> It is of high importance that judges constituting a court of last resort should use effort and self-restraint to promote solidarity of conclusions and the consequent influence of judicial decision. A judge should not yield to the pride of opinion or value more highly his individual reputation than that of the court to which he should be loyal. Except in case of conscientious difference of opinion on fundamental principle, dissenting opinions should be discouraged in courts of last resort. (Witkin 1977, 219, quoting Canon 19 of the ABA Canons of Judicial Ethics)

Despite this advice against writing concurrences and dissents, Supreme Court justices have increasingly issued concurring and dissenting opinions over the last fifty years. Even when a justice agrees with the disposition of the majority opinion, he or she frequently writes or joins a concurring opinion that seeks to limit, expand, clarify, or change the grounds for that opinion. In fact, Chief Justice John Marshall, concerned with providing legitimacy to the Court, discouraged separate opinions and many believe this contributed to building the Court's power and prestige.

There are valid reasons for writing or joining a separate opinion, such as to assure counsel and the public that the case has received careful consideration, to help reach a just result through careful formulation and application of a system of legal principles, to warn that the doctrine being laid down must not be pressed too far, and, by their threat, to improve craftsmanship in opinions by causing the writer to scrutinize them carefully for defects (Moorhead 1952).

However,

> [i]f a concurring ... opinion is not written with full respect for the doctrine of *stare decisis*, it serves neither to improve our jurisprudence nor to afford a reliable basis for prediction. ... [E]volution rather than revolution should be the rule. If the decisions of a court are consistently accompanied by concurring ... opinions

which represent attempts to substitute the impulses of the present for the wisdom of the past, the law suffers, and the only possible prediction is one of chaos. (Moorhead 1952, 884)

In this book, I have attempted to better understand decision making and opinion writing on the Supreme Court. Although scholarly attention is beginning to address this area, most research in judicial politics continues to center on case outcomes. Epstein and Kobylka (1992, 302), however, show that "the law and legal arguments grounded in law matter, and they matter dearly." Additionally, "to understand fully the political dynamics of the Court, we need to move beyond a study of voting alignments to explore the multiple strategies that produce Court opinions" (Maltzman, et al. 2000, 5), thus, it is important to study the content of Court opinions and how the opinions are crafted. This book has made a small step in that direction by analyzing concurrences, specifically answering two key questions:

1. Why does a justice write or join a particular type of concurring opinion rather than silently joining the majority?
2. What impact do published concurrences have?

The analysis throughout this book demonstrates that concurrences are the perfect vehicle in which the justices can communicate their understanding of the majority opinion. The concurrences that bracket the majority opinion provide information to other actors about what the case means, about how far the rationale can be extended to other cases, and about how much support the rationale of the majority opinion has. Although previous literature merged concurrences with dissents or treated concurrences equally, my overarching argument in this book is that concurrences are not the same and that justices use concurrences to communicate and to send signals to each other, the legal community, and the public. Only by analyzing the content of concurrences are we able to better understand the decision making and opinion writing process that occurs on the Supreme Court.

In order to analyze the content of concurrences, I coded them into the following different types: expansive, doctrinal, limiting, reluctant, emphatic, and unnecessary. I also provided a qualitative analysis of the bargaining and accommodation that occurs on the Supreme Court in order to understand why some concurrences are published and other "potential" concurrences are not. Finally, I assessed the impact that different types of concurring opinions have on lower court compliance and on the Supreme Court's interpretation of its own precedent, and found that concurrences do matter. In order to understand the impact of concurrences, one must understand what type of concurrence is being written.

In the data I analyzed, although a majority of the concurrences are expressing disagreement in some fashion with the majority opinion, 25 percent of the concurrences are quite supportive of the majority decision. This demonstrates that scholars who have treated all concurrences as disagreement are missing important differences and variations among the justices' behavior.

By performing a multivariate analysis with the type of concurrence as the dependent variable, I found that the decision to write or join a particular type of concurrence is a complex decision that involves justice-specific, case-specific, and institutional factors. The factors that influence a justice's decision whether to write or join a concurrence are different depending on the type of concurrence and what type of signal the justice wants to send. Thus, the empirical results illustrate the value of separating concurrences into different types. In short, all concurrences are not the same. Some concurrences support the majority decision, whereas others do not. Some concurrences contract the majority decision while others expand the reach of the majority decision.

I found a great deal of bargaining and accommodation between Blackmun and Marshall and the other justices during the 1986 to 1989 terms. The majority opinion of the Court is a collective document, the contents of which are reached by a great deal of bargaining and accommodation. I found that when a justice attempted to bargain with Blackmun or Marshall, more likely than not the justice was successful even when the justices were ideologically opposed. This book does not definitively answer why, given the high rate of success reached by most of the justices, there were not more attempts at bargaining by those who ended up writing or joining a concurrence. Perhaps the justices make strategic calculations, bargaining only when they believe they will be successful, based on the change they want and who the majority opinion writer is. This would account for the high success rate even by justices who were ideologically distant from Blackmun or Marshall as well as the instances in which the justices did not attempt to bargain with Blackmun or Marshall, even though they were not completely satisfied with the opinion and ultimately wrote or joined a concurring opinion.

It is clear that the justices do act strategically during the opinion writing process. Cooperating with justices is important, as is having a unanimous Court or needing five justices to sign on to the majority opinion. Justices also are influenced by the institution in which they find themselves, taking into account future interpretations by the legal community. They take their roles seriously. Although I cannot generalize beyond the behavior of Blackmun and Marshall, a picture emerges about the bargaining process that one is not able to obtain from previous studies. The majority of previous studies of the bargaining process on the Court relied on aggregate data. Moreover, most of the quantitative work does not link instances of bargaining with the specific accommodation that was made or rejected by the opinion author. Only by delving into the memos and analyzing their content is one able to discern the true level of bargaining and accommodation that occurs on the Supreme Court. Future work could analyze different justices to see if Blackmun and Marshall were more or less accommodating.

This study also addressed the following question: What impact do published concurrences have? Specifically, are lower courts more likely to treat Supreme Court precedent negatively when the case is accompanied by a concurrence? In the past, a debate has centered on whether concurrences serve any useful purpose or whether they shake the public's confidence in the Court.

> [C]oncurring and dissenting opinions are to be deplored if they result from personal rivalry or enmity among the members of a court, or if they are products of bemused reasoning or of a lack of judicial experience or temperament. With equal certainty, such an opinion should be condemned if it springs from a desire to indulge in judicial legislation; if it is an attempt to make an *ad hoc* disposition of a case according to its writer's individual concept of justice; or if, regardless of precedent, it is born in a preconceived political or economic philosophy. However, no criticism can justly be directed at an opinion which is motivated by honest conviction, which respects the doctrine of *stare decisis*—even though it might urge the overruling of a particular precedent—but which expresses a sincere belief that the court employed the wrong rationale or arrived at an erroneous result. (Moorhead 1952, 822)

By differentiating between the types of concurrences, this study illuminates the true impact they have on whether or not a lower court complies with the Supreme Court case. We now know that concurrences matter. Doctrinal concurrences negatively impact lower court compliance, whereas expansive concurrences positively impact lower court compliance. Thus, the justices of the Supreme Court, through writing and joining concurrences, have the potential to influence the impact that the majority decision has on the lower courts. When a Supreme Court justice makes the decision to write a particular type of concurrence, perhaps because bargaining between that justice and the majority opinion writer broke down, he or she is in a position to strengthen or weaken the impact of that majority decision. The justice wants to communicate something and that choice to communicate, to send a particular signal to the lower courts, actually does result in either a positive or negative impact. Although this book does not provide evidence that these signals are sent intentionally in an effort to affect the evolution of the law by the lower courts either interpreting the precedent in a positive or negative way, the evidence does show that, whether they are meant to or not, concurrences do influence the future interpretation of the precedent. Even if they are not purposely sending signals, the result is still the same: concurrences that offer stronger support for the precedent are more likely to be positively interpreted in the future, and concurrences that offer stronger disagreement with the precedent are more likely to be negatively interpreted in the future.

In order to be an effective governing institution, the Court must have legitimacy in the eyes of the public and other branches of government, relying on these other actors to turn the law into action. The Court also must rely on lower federal courts to interpret and implement its decisions. If the lower courts do not follow Supreme Court precedent, the impact the Court has on the public is weakened. If the lower courts follow Supreme Court precedent, the impact the Court has on the public is increased. Consequently, concurrences provide the justices with a tool to effectuate their policy preferences.

Finally, I addressed whether the choice to write or join a particular type of concurrence influences how the Supreme Court interprets its own precedent. I found that a precedent accompanied by an expansive concurrence increases the likelihood that the Supreme Court will positively treat the precedent while a precedent accompanied by a doctrinal concurrence decreases the likelihood that the Supreme Court will positively treat the precedent. This is consistent with the results obtained regarding compliance by the lower courts with Supreme Court precedent, indicating that the Supreme Court and the Circuit Courts of Appeals are reacting to the types of concurrences in a similar way. These findings provide support for the argument that, in addition to concurrences being used to signal to the lower court judges how to interpret and understand the majority opinion, the justices also use concurrences to communicate their understanding and support of the majority decision to each other.

By studying the process of opinion writing and the formation of legal doctrine through focusing on concurrences, this book provides a richer and more complete portrait of judicial decision making. When justices write or join a concurring opinion, they demonstrate that they have preferences over substantive legal rules. The justices care about the ends *and* the means. Concurrences provide a way for the justices to express their views about the law, and to engage in a dialogue of law with each other, the legal community, the public, and Congress. By focusing on case outcomes, important variation between the justices is obscured. For example, a justice may be labeled as a conservative, but how conservative? A justice may agree with the result, but does the justice agree with the reasoning? In the future, scholars need to consider not only case outcomes, but content. Future research could address the content of majority opinions, perhaps even scaling the opinions on a liberal-conservative continuum and coding concurrences in relation to the majority opinion. This study reinforces the point that "explorations of the Supreme Court should not begin and end with examinations of the vote, as they have for so many years. Rather, we must explore the range of choices that contribute to the development of the law" (Epstein and Knight 1998, 185). One of those choices is whether to write or join a concurring opinion.

Appendix

Table A.1. List of Cases, the Type of Concurrence, and the Justice Writing the Concurrence

Case	Justice Writing	Type of Concurrence
Colorado v. Connelly, 479 U.S. 157 (1986)	Blackmun	Limiting
Federal Elections Commission v. Massachusetts Citizens for Life, 479 U.S. 238 (1986)	O'Connor	Limiting
California Federal Savings & Loan Association v. Guerra, 479 U.S. 272 (1987)	Scalia	Limiting
California Federal Savings & Loan Association v. Guerra, 479 U.S. 272 (1987)	Stevens	Reluctant
Griffith v. Kentucky, 479 U.S. 314 (1987)	Powell	Expansive
Colorado v. Bertine, 479 U.S. 367 (1987)	Blackmun	Emphatic
Clarke v. Securities Industry Association, 479 U.S. 388 (1987)	Stevens	Limiting
Connecticut v. Barrett, 479 U.S. 523 (1987)	Brennan	Doctrinal
California v. Brown, 479 U.S. 538 (1987)	O'Connor	Emphatic
Pennsylvania v. Ritchie, 480 U.S. 39 (1987)	Blackmun	Doctrinal
Asahi Metal Industry Co. v. Superior Court of California, 480 U.S. 102 (1987)	Stevens	Limiting
Asahi Metal Industry Co. v. Superior Court of California, 480 U.S. 102 (1987)	Brennan	Doctrinal
Western Air Lines v. Board of Equalization, 480 U.S. 123 (1987)	White	Limiting
Hobbie v. Unemployment Appeals Commission, 480 U.S. 136 (1987)	Powell	Limiting
Hobbie v. Unemployment Appeals Commission, 480 U.S. 136 (1987)	Stevens	Emphatic

Case	Justice	Category
FCC v. Florida Power Corp., 480 U.S. 245 (1987)	Powell	Emphatic
United States v. Dunn, 480 U.S. 294 (1987)	Scalia	Doctrinal
Arizona v. Hicks, 480 U.S. 321 (1987)	White	Emphatic
Stringfellow v. Concerned Neighbors, 480 U.S. 370 (1987)	Brennan	Doctrinal
Newton v. Rumery, 480 U.S. 386 (1987)	O'Connor	Limiting
INS v. Cardoza-Fonseca, 480 U.S. 421 (1987)	Scalia	Limiting
INS v. Cardoza-Fonseca, 480 U.S. 421 (1987)	Blackmun	Emphatic
Amoco Prod. Co. v. Vill. Of Gambell, 480 U.S. 531 (1987)	Stevens	Limiting
Johnson v. Transportation Agency, 480 U.S. 616 (1987)	Stevens	Emphatic
Johnson v. Transportation Agency, 480 U.S. 616 (1987)	O'Connor	Doctrinal
Penzoil Co v. Texaco Inc., 481 U.S. 1 (1987)	Scalia	Expansive
Penzoil Co v. Texaco Inc., 481 U.S. 1 (1987)	Marshall	Doctrinal
Penzoil Co v. Texaco Inc., 481 U.S. 1 (1987)	Brennan	Doctrinal
Penzoil Co v. Texaco Inc., 481 U.S. 1 (1987)	Blackmun	Doctrinal
Penzoil Co v. Texaco Inc., 481 U.S. 1 (1987)	Stevens	Doctrinal
Metropolitan Life Ins. Co v. Taylor, 481 U.S. 58 (1987)	Brennan	Limiting
CTS Corp. v. Dynamics Corp. of Am., 481 U.S. 69 (1987)	Scalia	Limiting
Arkansas Writers' Project, Inc. v. Ragland, 481 U.S. 221 (1987)	Stevens	Limiting
Pope v. Illinois, 481 U.S. 497 (1987)	Scalia	Reluctant
Board of Directors of Rotary Int'l v. Rotary Club of Duarte, 481 U.S. 537 (1987)	Scalia	Unnecessary
Pennsylvania v. Finley, 481 U.S. 551 (1987)	Blackmun	Expansive
NLRB v. International Bhd. Of Elec. Workers, Local 340, 481 U.S. 573 (1987)	Scalia	Limiting
St. Francis College v. Al-Khazraji, 481 U.S. 604 (1987)	Brennan	Emphatic
Rose v. Rose, 481 U.S. 619 (1987)	Scalia	Limiting
Rose v. Rose, 481 U.S. 619 (1987)	O'Connor	Doctrinal

Case	Justice	Category
Gray v. Mississippi, 481 U.S. 648 (1987)	Powell	Doctrinal
Hodel v. Irving, 481 U.S. 704 (1987)	Scalia	Emphatic
Hodel v. Irving, 481 U.S. 704 (1987)	Brennan	Emphatic
Hodel v. Irving, 481 U.S. 704 (1987)	Stevens	Doctrinal
Young v. United States, 481 U.S. 787 (1987)	Blackmun	Expansive
Young v. United States, 481 U.S. 787 (1987)	Scalia	Doctrinal
United States v. Hohri, 482 U.S. 64 (1987)	Blackmun	Reluctant
Bowen v. Yuckert, 482 U.S. 137 (1987)	O'Connor	Expansive
Interstate Commerce Com. v. Brotherhood of Locomotive Engineers, 482 U.S. 270 (1987)	Stevens	Doctrinal
Crawford Fitting Co. v. J.T. Gibbons Inc., 482 U.S. 437 (1987)	Blackmun	Limiting
Houston v. Hill, 482 U.S. 451 (1987)	Blackmun	Limiting
Houston v. Hill, 482 U.S. 451 (1987)	Scalia	Doctrinal
Board of Airport Comm'rs v. Jews for Jesus, 482 U.S. 569 (1987)	White	Expansive
Edwards v. Aguillard, 482 U.S. 578 (1987)	Powell	Emphatic
Edwards v. Aguillard, 482 U.S. 578 (1987)	White	Reluctant
Citicorp Industrial Credit, Inc. v. Brock, 483 U.S. 27 (1987)	Scalia	Limiting
Commissioner v. Fink, 483 U.S. 89 (1987)	White	Expansive
Commissioner v. Fink, 483 U.S. 89 (1987)	Scalia	Doctrinal
Commissioner v. Fink, 483 U.S. 89 (1987)	Blackmun	Unnecessary
Agency Holding Corp. v. Malley-Duff & Associates, Inc, 483 U.S. 143 (1987)	Scalia	Doctrinal
Bourjaily v. United States, 483 U.S. 171 (1987)	Stevens	Expansive
Puerto Rico v. Branstad, 483 U.S. 219 (1987)	O'Connor	Limiting
Puerto Rico v. Branstad, 483 U.S. 219 (1987)	Scalia	Limiting
Tyler Pipe Indus. v. Washington State Dep't. of Revenue, 483 U.S. 232 (1987)	O'Connor	Limiting
Corporation of Presiding Bishop of the Church of Jesus Christ of Latter-Day Saints v. Amos, 483 U.S. 327 (1987)	Brennan	Doctrinal

Corporation of Presiding Bishop of the Church of Jesus Christ of Latter-Day Saints v. Amos, 483 U.S. 327 (1987)	Blackmun	Doctrinal
Corporation of Presiding Bishop of the Church of Jesus Christ of Latter-Day Saints v. Amos, 483 U.S. 327 (1987)	O'Connor	Doctrinal
Rankin v. McPherson, 483 U.S. 378 (1987)	Powell	Limiting
Solorio v. United States, 483 U.S. 435 (1987)	Stevens	Limiting
Rivera v. Minnich, 483 U.S. 574 (1987)	O'Connor	Doctrinal
Greer v. Miller, 483 U.S. 756 (1987)	Stevens	Doctrinal
United Paperworkers International Union v. Misco, Inc., 484 U.S. 29 (1987)	Blackmun	Limiting
Gwaltney of Smithfield v. Chesapeake Bay Found., 484 U.S. 49 (1987)	Scalia	Doctrinal
NLRB v. United Food & Commercial Workers Union, Local 23, 484 U.S. 112 (1987)	Scalia	Emphatic
Thompson v. Thompson, 484 U.S. 174 (1988)	O'Connor	Limiting
Thompson v. Thompson, 484 U.S. 174 (1988)	Scalia	Doctrinal
Deakins v. Monaghan, 484 U.S. 193 (1988)	White	Doctrinal
Honig v. Doe, 484 U.S. 305 (1988)	Rehnquist	Expansive
United States v. Fausto, 484 U.S. 439 (1988)	Blackmun	Emphatic
Hustler Magazine v. Falwell, 485 U.S. 46 (1988)	White	Doctrinal
Mathews v. United States, 485 U.S. 58 (1988)	Brennan	Reluctant
Mathews v. United States, 485 U.S. 58 (1988)	Scalia	Doctrinal
Gulfstream Aerospace Corp. v. Mayacamas Corp., 485 U.S. 271 (1988)	Scalia	Expansive
Boos v. Barry, 485 U.S. 312 (1988)	Brennan	Doctrinal
Tulsa Professional Collection Services, Inc. v. Pope, 485 U.S. 478 (1988)	Blackmun	Unnecessary
South Carolina v. Baker, 485 U.S. 505 (1988)	Rehnquist	Limiting
South Carolina v. Baker, 485 U.S. 505 (1988)	Scalia	Limiting
South Carolina v. Baker, 485 U.S. 505 (1988)	Stevens	Emphatic
Edward J. DeBartolo Corp. v. Florida Gulf Coast Bldg, 485 U.S. 568 (1988)	Scalia, O'Connor	Unnecessary
Regents of Univ. of California v. Public Employment Relations Bd., 485 U.S. 589 (1988)	White	Doctrinal

Appendix

Case	Justice	Type
Kungys v. United States, 485 U.S. 759 (1988)	Stevens	Doctrinal
Kungys v. United States, 485 U.S. 759 (1988)	Brennan	Emphatic
Bankers Life & Casualty Co. v. Crenshaw, 486 U.S. 71 (1988)	White	Doctrinal
Bankers Life & Casualty Co. v. Crenshaw, 486 U.S. 71 (1988)	O'Connor	Doctrinal
Bankers Life & Casualty Co. v. Crenshaw, 486 U.S. 71 (1988)	Scalia	Doctrinal
EEOC v. Commercial Office Products Co., 486 U.S. 107 (1988)	O'Connor	Limiting
Chick Kam Choo v. Exxon Corp., 486 U.S. 140 (1988)	White	Reluctant
Satterwhite v. Texas, 486 U.S. 249 (1988)	Marshall	Doctrinal
Satterwhite v. Texas, 486 U.S. 249 (1988)	Blackmun	Doctrinal
Maynard v. Cartwright, 486 U.S. 356 (1988)	Brennan	Expansive
Mills v. Maryland, 486 U.S. 367 (1988)	Brennan	Expansive
Mills v. Maryland, 486 U.S. 367 (1988)	White	Emphatic
Michigan v. Chesternut, 486 U.S. 567 (1988)	Kennedy	Expansive
Johnson v. Mississippi, 486 U.S. 578 (1988)	Brennan	Expansive
Johnson v. Mississippi, 486 U.S. 578 (1988)	White	Emphatic
Johnson v. Mississippi, 486 U.S. 578 (1988)	O'Connor	Unnecessary
Volkswagenwerk Aktiengesellschaft v. Schlunk, 486 U.S. 694 (1988)	Brennan	Doctrinal
Sun Oil Co. v. Wortman, 486 U.S. 717 (1988)	Brennan	Doctrinal
Christianson v. Colt Industries Operating Corp., 486 U.S. 800 (1988)	Stevens	Expansive
I.N.S. v. Pangilinan, 486 U.S. 875 (1988)	Blackmun	Unnecessary
Bendix Autolite Corp. v. Midwesco Enterprises, Inc., 486 U.S. 888 (1988)	Scalia	Doctrinal
N.Y. State Club Ass'n. v. City of New York, 487 U.S. 1 (1988)	O'Connor	Limiting
N.Y. State Club Ass'n. v. City of New York, 487 U.S. 1 (1988)	Scalia	Limiting
Stewart Org., Inc. v. Ricoh Corp., 487 U.S. 22 (1988)	Kennedy	Expansive

West v. Atkins, 487 U.S. 42 (1988)	Scalia	Doctrinal
Felder v. Casey, 487 U.S. 131 (1988)	White	Expansive
Bank of Nova Scotia v. United States, 487 U.S. 250 (1988)	Scalia	Limiting
Torres v. Oakland Scavenger Co., 487 U.S. 312 (1988)	Scalia	Doctrinal
United States v. Taylor, 487 U.S. 326 (1988)	Scalia	Limiting
United States v. Taylor, 487 U.S. 326 (1988)	White	Emphatic
Mississippi Power & Light Co. v. Mississippi, 487 U.S. 354 (1988)	Scalia	Doctrinal
Sheridan v. United States, 487 U.S. 392 (1988)	Kennedy	Doctrinal
Sheridan v. United States, 487 U.S. 392 (1988)	White	Emphatic
Schweiker v. Chilicky, 487 U.S. 412 (1988)	Stevens	Expansive
Frisby v. Schultz, 487 U.S. 474 (1988)	White	Doctrinal
Pierce v. Underwood, 487 U.S. 552 (1988)	Brennan	Doctrinal
Bowen v. Kendrick, 487 U.S. 589 (1988)	O'Connor	Expansive
Bowen v. Kendrick, 487 U.S. 589 (1988)	Kennedy	Limiting
Riley v. National Federation of Blind, Inc, 487 U.S. 781 (1988)	Scalia	Doctrinal
Bowen v. Massachusetts, 487 U.S. 879 (1988)	White	Doctrinal
United States v. Kozminski, 487 U.S. 931 (1988)	Brennan	Doctrinal
United States v. Kozminski, 487 U.S. 931 (1988)	Stevens	Doctrinal
Watson v. Ft. Worth Bank & Trust, 487 U.S. 977 (1988)	Stevens	Limiting
Watson v. Ft. Worth Bank & Trust, 487 U.S. 977 (1988)	Blackmun	Doctrinal
Coy v. Iowa, 487 U.S. 1012 (1988)	O'Connor	Limiting
Arizona v. Youngblood, 488 U.S. 51 (1988)	Stevens	Limiting
Penson v. Ohio, 488 U.S. 75 (1988)	O'Connor	Limiting
Bowen v. Georgetown Univ. Hosp., 488 U.S. 204 (1988)	Scalia	Expansive
Goldberg v. Sweet, 488 U.S. 252 (1989)	Stevens	Doctrinal
Goldberg v. Sweet, 488 U.S. 252 (1989)	O'Connor	Doctrinal
Goldberg v. Sweet, 488 U.S. 252 (1989)	Scalia	Doctrinal

Perry v. Leeke, 488 U.S. 272 (1989)	Kennedy	Limiting
Duquesne Light Co. v. Barasch, 488 U.S. 299 (1989)	Scalia	Expansive
Reed v. United Transp. Union, 488 U.S. 319 (1989)	Scalia	Limiting
Sheet Metal Workers' Int'l Ass'n v. Lynn, 488 U.S. 347 (1989)	White	Doctrinal
Argentine Republic v. Amerada Hess Shipping Corp., 488 U.S. 428 (1989)	Blackmun	Limiting
Richmond v. J.A. Croson Co., 488 U.S. 469 (1989)	Stevens	Doctrinal
Richmond v. J.A. Croson Co., 488 U.S. 469 (1989)	Scalia	Doctrinal
Richmond v. J.A. Croson Co., 488 U.S. 469 (1989)	Kennedy	Emphatic
United States v. Broce, 488 U.S. 563 (1989)	Stevens	Expansive
Ft. Wayne Books v. Indiana, 489 U.S. 46 (1989)	Blackmun	Reluctant
Blanchard v. Bergeron, 489 U.S. 87 (1989)	Scalia	Doctrinal
Firestone Tire & Rubber Co. v. Bruch, 489 U.S. 101 (1989)	Scalia	Doctrinal
Mesa v. California, 489 U.S. 121 (1989)	Brennan	Emphatic
Eu v. San Fransisco County Democratic Cent. Comm., 489 U.S. 214 (1989)	Stevens	Limiting
Harris v. Reed, 489 U.S. 255 (1989)	Stevens	Limiting
Harris v. Reed, 489 U.S. 255 (1989)	O'Connor	Limiting
Teague v. Lane, 489 U.S. 288 (1989)	White	Reluctant
Teague v. Lane, 489 U.S. 288 (1989)	Blackmun	Doctrinal
Teague v. Lane, 489 U.S. 288 (1989)	Stevens	Doctrinal
United States v. Stuart, 489 U.S. 353 (1989)	Scalia	Limiting
United States v. Stuart, 489 U.S. 353 (1989)	Kennedy	Limiting
City of Canton v. Harris, 489 U.S. 378 (1989)	Brennan	Emphatic
Colt Independence Joint Venture v. Federal Sav. & Loan Ins. Corp., 489 U.S. 561 (1989)	Blackmun	Limiting
Colt Independence Joint Venture v. Federal Sav. & Loan Ins. Corp., 489 U.S. 561 (1989)	Scalia	Limiting
Brower v. County of Inyo, 489 U.S. 593 (1989)	Stevens	Limiting

Case	Justice	Category
Skinner v. Railway Labor Executives Ass'n, 489 U.S. 602 (1989)	Stevens	Limiting
Board of Estimate v. Morris, 489 U.S. 688 (1989)	Brennan	Limiting
Board of Estimate v. Morris, 489 U.S. 688 (1989)	Blackmun	Limiting
United States DOJ v. Reporters Comm. for Freedom of Press, 489 U.S. 749 (1989)	Blackmun	Doctrinal
Dallas v. Stanglin, 490 U.S. 19 (1989)	Stevens	Doctrinal
Amerada Hess Corp. v. Director, Div. of Taxation, New Jersey Dep't of Treasury, 490 U.S. 66 (1989)	Scalia	Limiting
Chan v. Korean Air Lines, Ltd., 490 U.S. 122 (1989)	Brennan	Doctrinal
Mallard v. United States Dist. Court for Southern Dist., 490 U.S. 296 (1989)	Kennedy	Emphatic
Robertson v. Methow Valley Citizens Council, 490 U.S. 332 (1989)	Brennan	Emphatic
Graham v. Connor, 490 U.S. 386 (1989)	Blackmun	Limiting
United States v. Halper, 490 U.S. 435 (1989)	Kennedy	Limiting
Kentucky Dep't of Corrections v. Thompson, 490 U.S. 454 (1989)	Kennedy	Limiting
Lauro Lines s.r.l. v. Chasser, 490 U.S. 495 (1989)	Scalia	Expansive
Green v. Bock Laundry Mach. Co., 490 U.S. 504 (1989)	Scalia	Doctrinal
ASARCO, Inc. v. Kadish, 490 U.S. 605 (1989)	Brennan	Limiting
South Carolina v. Gathers, 490 U.S. 805 (1989)	White	Reluctant
Lorance v. AT&T Technologies, 490 U.S. 900 (1989)	Stevens	Reluctant
Pennsylvania v. Union Gas Co., 491 U.S. 1 (1989)	Stevens	Expansive
Dellmuth v. Muth, 491 U.S. 223 (1989)	Scalia	Emphatic
Consolidated Rail Corp. v. Railway Labor Executives' Ass'n, 491 U.S. 299 (1989)	White	Emphatic
Healy v. Beer Inst., 491 U.S. 324 (1989)	Scalia	Limiting
New Orleans Public Service, Inc. v. New Orleans, 491 U.S. 350 (1989)	Brennan	Limiting
New Orleans Public Service, Inc. v. New Orleans, 491 U.S. 350 (1989)	Blackmun	Limiting

Appendix

New Orleans Public Service, Inc. v. New Orleans, 491 U.S. 350 (1989)	Rehnquist	Limiting
Texas v. Johnson, 491 U.S. 397 (1989)	Kennedy	Reluctant
Public Citizen v. United States Dep't of Justice, 491 U.S. 440 (1989)	Kennedy	Doctrinal
Florida Star v. B.J.F., 491 U.S. 524 (1989)	Scalia	Limiting
Harte-Hanks Communications, Inc. v. Connaughton, 491 U.S. 657 (1989)	Blackmun	Expansive
Harte-Hanks Communications, Inc. v. Connaughton, 491 U.S. 657 (1989)	Kennedy	Expansive
Harte-Hanks Communications, Inc. v. Connaughton, 491 U.S. 657 (1989)	White	Emphatic
Harte-Hanks Communications, Inc. v. Connaughton, 491 U.S. 657 (1989)	Scalia	Doctrinal
Jett v. Dallas Indep. Sch. Dist., 491 U.S. 701 (1989)	Scalia	Limiting
Independent Fed'n of Flight Attendants v. Zipes, 491 U.S. 754 (1989)	Blackmun	Doctrinal
Ward v. Rock Against Racism, 491 U.S. 781 (1989)	Blackmun	Unnecessary
Granfinanciera, S.A. v. Nordberg, 492 U.S. 33 (1989)	Scalia	Doctrinal
Sable Communications of California, Inc. v. FCC, 492 U.S. 115 (1989)	Scalia	Limiting
U.S. Department of Justice v. Tax Analysts, 492 U.S. 136 (1989)	White	Unnecessary
Duckworth v. Eagan, 492 U.S. 195 (1989)	O'Connor	Expansive
H.J., Inc. v. Northwestern Bell Tel. Co., 492 U.S. 229 (1989)	Scalia	Doctrinal
Browning-Ferris Indus. v. Kelco Disposal, Inc., 492 U.S. 257 (1989)	Brennan	Reluctant
Stanford v. Kentucky, 492 U.S. 361 (1989)	O'Connor	Doctrinal
Webster v. Reproductive Health Services, 492 U.S. 490 (1989)	O'Connor	Limiting
Webster v. Reproductive Health Services, 492 U.S. 490 (1989)	Scalia	Expansive

Appendix

Case	Justice	Type
County of Allegheny v. American Civil Liberties Union, Greater Pittsburgh Chapter, 492 U.S. 573 (1989)	O'Connor	Doctrinal
Chesapeake & O. Ry. v. Schwalb, 493 U.S. 40 (1989)	Blackmun	Limiting
Chesapeake & O. Ry. v. Schwalb, 493 U.S. 40 (1989)	Stevens	Reluctant
John Doe Agency v. John Doe Corp., 493 U.S. 146 (1989)	Brennan	Limiting
James v. Illinois, 493 U.S. 307 (1990)	Stevens	Expansive
Tafflin v. Levitt, 493 U.S. 455 (1990)	White	Limiting
Tafflin v. Levitt, 493 U.S. 455 (1990)	Scalia	Limiting
Holland v. Illinois, 493 U.S. 474 (1990)	Kennedy	Limiting
Preseault v. ICC, 494 U.S. 1 (1990)	O'Connor	Expansive
Reves v. Ernst & Young, 494 U.S. 56 (1990)	Stevens	Expansive
Crandon v. United States, 494 U.S. 152 (1990)	Scalia	Doctrinal
Washington v. Harper, 494 U.S. 210 (1990)	Blackmun	Emphatic
United States v. Verdugo-Urquidez, 494 U.S. 259 (1990)	Kennedy	Expansive
United States v. Verdugo-Urquidez, 494 U.S. 259 (1990)	Stevens	Doctrinal
Maryland v. Buie, 494 U.S. 325 (1990)	Stevens	Limiting
Maryland v. Buie, 494 U.S. 325 (1990)	Kennedy	Emphatic
McKoy v. North Carolina, 494 U.S. 433 (1990)	Kennedy	Limiting
McKoy v. North Carolina, 494 U.S. 433 (1990)	Blackmun	Expansive
McKoy v. North Carolina, 494 U.S. 433 (1990)	White	Emphatic
Lytle v. Household Mfg., Inc., 494 U.S. 545 (1990)	O'Connor	Emphatic
Chauffeurs, Teamsters & Helpers, Local No. 391 v. Terry, 494 U.S. 558 (1990)	Brennan	Doctrinal
Chauffeurs, Teamsters & Helpers, Local No. 391 v. Terry, 494 U.S. 558 (1990)	Stevens	Doctrinal
Butterworth v. Smith, 494 U.S. 624 (1990)	Scalia	Limiting
Austin v. Mich. State Chamber of Commerce, 494 U.S. 652 (1990)	Brennan	Expansive
Austin v. Mich. State Chamber of Commerce, 494 U.S. 652 (1990)	Stevens	Expansive

United States Dep't. of Labor v Triplett, 494 U.S. 715 (1990)	Marshall	Limiting
United States Dep't. of Labor v Triplett, 494 U.S. 715 (1990)	Brennan	Limiting
United States Dep't. of Labor v Triplett, 494 U.S. 715 (1990)	Stevens	Limiting
NLRB v. Curtin Matheson Scientific, Inc., 494 U.S. 775 (1990)	Rehnquist	Limiting
Kaiser Aluminum & Chem. Corp. v. Bonjorno, 494 U.S. 827 (1990)	Scalia	Expansive
Employment Div. v. Smith, 494 U.S. 872 (1990)	O'Connor	Doctrinal
Florida v. Wells, 495 U.S. 1 (1990)	Brennan	Limiting
Florida v. Wells, 495 U.S. 1 (1990)	Blackmun	Limiting
Florida v. Wells, 495 U.S. 1 (1990)	Stevens	Limiting
Minnesota v. Olson, 495 U.S. 91 (1990)	Stevens	Limiting
Minnesota v. Olson, 495 U.S. 91 (1990)	Kennedy	Limiting
Osborne v. Ohio, 495 U.S. 103 (1990)	Blackmun	Emphatic
Stewart v. Abend, 495 U.S. 207 (1990)	White	Reluctant
United States v. Ojeda Rios, 495 U.S. 257 (1990)	O'Connor	Emphatic
California v. Am. Stores Co., 495 U.S. 271 (1990)	Kennedy	Expansive
Port Auth. Trans-Hudson Corp. v. Feeney, 495 U.S. 299 (1990)	Brennan	Doctrinal
United States v. Munoz-Flores, 495 U.S. 385 (1990)	Stevens	Doctrinal
United States v. Munoz-Flores, 495 U.S. 385 (1990)	Scalia	Doctrinal
Taylor v. United States, 495 U.S. 575 (1990)	Scalia	Limiting
Ft. Stewart Schools v. FLRA, 495 U.S. 641 (1990)	Marshall	Limiting
Citibank, N.A. v. Wells Fargo Asia, Ltd., 495 U.S. 660 (1990)	Rehnquist	Reluctant
Begier v. IRS, 496 U.S. 53 (1990)	Scalia	Doctrinal
Board of Educ. of Westside Community Schools v. Mergens, 496 U.S. 226 (1990)	Marshall	Doctrinal
Board of Educ. of Westside Community Schools v. Mergens, 496 U.S. 226 (1990)	Kennedy	Doctrinal
Illinois v. Perkins, 496 U.S. 292 (1990)	Brennan	Limiting
OPM v. Richmond, 496 U.S. 414 (1990)	White	Limiting

Appendix

OPM v. Richmond, 496 U.S. 414 (1990)	Stevens	Doctrinal
Michigan Dep't of State Police v. Sitz, 496 U.S. 444 (1990)	Blackmun	Emphatic
Texaco, Inc. v. Hasbrouck, 496 U.S. 543 (1990)	White	Limiting
Texaco, Inc. v. Hasbrouck, 496 U.S. 543 (1990)	Scalia	Doctrinal
Sullivan v. Finkelstein, 496 U.S. 617 (1990)	Scalia	Limiting
Sullivan v. Finkelstein, 496 U.S. 617 (1990)	Blackmun	Doctrinal
Collins v. Youngblood, 497 U.S. 37 (1990)	Stevens	Doctrinal
Rutan v. Republican Party, 497 U.S. 62 (1990)	Stevens	Expansive
Maislin Indus., U.S. v. Primary Steel, 497 U.S. 116 (1990)	Scalia	Expansive
Portland Golf Club v. Commissioner, 497 U.S. 154 (1990)	Kennedy	Doctrinal
Cruzan v. Director, Missouri Dep't of Health, 497 U.S. 261 (1990)	O'Connor	Limiting
Cruzan v. Director, Missouri Dep't of Health, 497 U.S. 261 (1990)	Scalia	Limiting
Sisson v. Ruby, 497 U.S. 358 (1990)	Scalia	Doctrinal
Ohio v. Akron Ctr. for Reproductive Health, 497 U.S. 502 (1990)	Stevens	Limiting
Ohio v. Akron Ctr. for Reproductive Health, 497 U.S. 502 (1990)	Scalia	Expansive
Metro Broadcasting, Inc. v. FCC, 497 U.S. 547 (1990)	Stevens	Emphatic
Walton v. Arizona, 497 U.S. 639 (1990)	Scalia	Doctrinal

Table A.2. Multinomial Logit Model of Justices' Decisions to Write or Join a Specific Type of Concurrence Versus Joining the Majority Opinion (1986–1989 Terms)

Variable	Limiting	Reluctant	Expansive	Emphatic	Doctrinal	Unnecessary
Justice-Specific						
Ideological compatibility	-.104 (.106)	-.413 (.259)*	-.029 (.160)	.044 (.141)	.031 (.103)	.217 (.182)
Taught law	.571 (.207)***	.138 (.548)	.733 (.316)**	-.281 (.302)	.237 (.189)	.724 (.756)
Cooperation	-9.750 (2.855)***	-2.476 (2.517)	-.284 (.987)	-8.067 (3.607)**	-10.789 (5.173)**	-35.470 (12.431)***
Case-Specific						
Complexity	.219 (.103)**	-.838 (.737)	.078 (.176)	.232 (.139)**	.162 (.108)*	.005 (.465)
Political importance	.316 (.258)	.574 (.559)	.639 (.376)**	.738 (.363)**	.153 (.273)	.061 (1.071)
Legal importance	.743 (.277)***	.337 (.695)	.777 (.411)**	.457 (.439)	-.254 (.381)	.461 (1.071)
Minimum winning coalition	-.661 (.338)**	.169 (.671)	.076 (.380)	-.611 (.500)	-1.306 (.403)***	-29.700 (.421)***
Institutional						
Chief Justice	-.867 (.477)**	-.840 (1.074)	-.911 (.755)	-.650 (.540)	-2.158 (.727)***	-29.420 (.603)***
Freshman justice	-.406 (.199)**	-.580 (.540)	.044 (.306)	-.235 (.286)	.047 (.190)	.198 (.782)
Constant	-3.401 (.320)***	-3.017 (1.713)**	-4.619 (.528)***	-4.051 (.424)***	-2.950 (.321)***	-5.533 (1.572)***

N = 2,985

Wald χ^2-Squared =7990.18***

*$p < .10$, **$p < .05$, ***$p < .01$, one-tailed tests where directionality hypothesized. Robust standard errors are reported in parentheses.

Table A.3. Descriptive Statistics for Independent Variables in Multinomial Logit Model of Justices' Decisions to Write or Join a Specific Type of Concurrence Versus Joining the Majority Opinion (1986–1989 Terms)

Variable	Mean	Standard Deviation	Minimum	Maximum
Ideological compatibility	.069	1.011	−2	2
Taught law	.417	.493	0	1
Cooperation	.053	.127	0	.786
Complexity	2.395	.789	2	9
Politically important	.139	.346	0	1
Legally important	.081	.273	0	1
Minimum winning coalition	.161	.367	0	1
Chief justice	.120	.325	0	1
Freshman justice	.559	.497	0	1

Table A.4. Logit Model of the Impact of Concurrences on Treatment of Supreme Court Precedent in the Courts of Appeals

Variable	Coefficient	Robust Standard Error
Type of Concurrence		
Expansive	.651	.207***
Doctrinal	−.224	.157*
Limiting	.091	.142
Reluctant	.241	.436
Emphatic	−.109	.216
Unnecessary	−.903	.912
Control Variables		
Dissents	−.097	.084
Age	.036	.010***
Complexity	.080	.060
Ideological incompatibility	−.251	.156*
Political importance	.001	.138
Legal importance	−.779	.164***
Change in Supreme Court ideology	−1.530	.352***
Positive Supreme Court treatment	.235	.062***
Negative Supreme Court treatment	−.209	.098**
Overruled	−.906	.187***
Constant	.900	.286***

N = 2,712; Wald χ-Squared = 191.87***; Pseudo R^2 = .063.

*p < .10, **p < .05, ***p < .01 (one-tailed tests where directionality hypothesized).

Note: Fixed effects for each circuit are not reported.

Table A.5. Descriptive Statistics for Independent Variables in Logit Model of the Impact of Concurrences on Treatment of Supreme Court Precedent in the Courts of Appeals

Variable	Mean	Standard Deviation	Minimum	Maximum
Type of Concurrence				
Expansive	.074	.261	0	1
Doctrinal	.105	.307	0	1
Limiting	.139	.346	0	1
Reluctant	.011	.106	0	1
Emphatic	.060	.238	0	1
Unnecessary	.002	.043	0	1
No concurrence	.679	.467	0	1
Dissents	1.012	.681	0	3
Age	7.058	5.211	0	17
Complexity	2.821	.945	2	8
Ideological incompatibility	.413	.304	.003	1.313
Political importance	.209	.407	0	1
Legal importance	.077	.267	0	1
Change in Supreme Court ideology	.191	.151	0	.563
Positive Supreme Court treatment	.595	.997	0	5
Negative Supreme Court treatment	.282	.519	0	3
Overruled	.066	.248	0	1
First circuit	.046	.210	0	1
Second circuit	.056	.231	0	1
Third circuit	.070	.255	0	1
Fourth circuit	.060	.238	0	1
Fifth circuit	.093	.290	0	1
Sixth circuit	.105	.307	0	1
Seventh circuit	.099	.298	0	1
Eighth circuit	.083	.276	0	1
Ninth circuit	.176	.381	0	1
Tenth circuit	.090	.287	0	1
Eleventh circuit	.081	.273	0	1
DC circuit	.040	.196	0	1

Table A.6. Logit Model of the Impact of Multiple Concurrences on Treatment of Supreme Court Precedent in the Courts of Appeals

Variable	Coefficient	Robust Standard Error
Concurrences—Net Support	.112	.079*
Control Variables		
Dissents	-.094	.084
Age	.033	.010***
Complexity	.089	.058
Ideological consistency	-.175	.154
Political importance	-.053	.124
Legal importance	-.643	.159***
Change in Supreme Court ideology	-1.483	.345***
Positive Supreme Court treatment	.252	.063***
Negative Supreme Court treatment	-.235	.097***
Overruled	-.905	.184***
Constant	.911	.277***

N = 2,712; Wald χ-Squared = 173.96***; Pseudo R^2 = .06

*p < .10, **p < .05, ***p < .01 (one-tailed tests where directionality hypothesized).

Note: Fixed effects for each circuit are not reported.

Table A.7. Predicted Probabilities of Positive Treatment, by Circuit

	1st	2nd	3rd	4th	5th	6th	7th	8th	9th	10th	11th	DC
Baseline	.725	.691	.746	.867	.769	.825	.793	.734	.762	.803	.794	.737
Expansive concurrence	.835	.811	.850	.926	.865	.900	.880	.841	.860	.886	.881	.843
Doctrinal concurrence	.678	.641	.702	.839	.727	.790	.754	.688	.719	.765	.755	.691
Minimum age of Supreme Court precedent (0)	.671	.634	.695	.835	.721	.785	.748	.681	.713	.759	.749	.685
Maximum age of Supreme Court precedent (17)	.790	.762	.808	.903	.827	.871	.845	.798	.821	.853	.846	.800
Legally important Supreme Court precedent	.547	.506	.575	.750	.604	.683	.637	.559	.595	.651	.639	.562
Minimum level of ideological compatibility (1.313)	.677	.641	.701	.839	.727	.790	.753	.687	.718	.764	.754	.691
Maximum level of ideological compatibility (.0026)	.745	.712	.765	.879	.787	.839	.809	.753	.780	.819	.810	.756
Minimum level of change in Supreme Court ideology (0)	.779	.750	.798	.897	.817	.863	.837	.787	.811	.845	.838	.789
Maximum level of change in Supreme Court ideology (.563)	.598	.558	.625	.787	.653	.727	.684	.609	.644	.697	.685	.613
Minimum number of positive treatments by Supreme Court (0)	.696	.660	.719	.850	.743	.803	.769	.706	.735	.780	.770	.709
Maximum number of positive treatments by Supreme Court (5)	.881	.863	.892	.949	.904	.930	.915	.886	.900	.920	.916	.888
Minimum number of negative treatments by Supreme Court (0)	.736	.703	.757	.874	.779	.833	.802	.745	.772	.812	.803	.748
Maximum number of negative treatments by Supreme Court (3)	.598	.559	.625	.787	.653	.727	.684	.610	.644	.697	.686	.613
Overruled Supreme Court precedent	.515	.475	.543	.725	.574	.655	.607	.527	.564	.622	.609	.531

Table A.8. Logit Model of the Impact of Type of Concurrence on Positive Treatment of Supreme Court Precedent by the Supreme Court

Variable	Coefficient	Robust Standard Error
Type of Concurrence		
Expansive	2.942	1.080***
Doctrinal	−1.537	.692**
Limiting	−.573	.630
Reluctant	.584	1.125
Emphatic	.150	.718
Control Variables		
Number of Dissents	−.233	.295
Age of precedent	−.043	.043
Complexity	.114	.221
Ideological incompatibility between Supreme Court and precedent	−.190	.135*
Political importance	−.543	.602
Legal importance	−2.064	.757***
Net positive Supreme Court Treatment	.019	.241
Overruled	1.115	1.211
Constant	.801	.770

$N = 135$; Wald χ-Squared = 22.38*; Pseudo R^2 = .142

*p < .10, **p < .05, ***p < .01 (one-tailed tests where directionality hypothesized).

Table A.9. Descriptive Statistics for Independent Variables in Logit Model of the Impact of the Type of Concurrence on Positive Treatment of Supreme Court Precedent by the Supreme Court

Variable	Mean	Standard Deviation	Minimum	Maximum
Type of Concurrence				
Expansive	.074	.263	0	1
Doctrinal	.104	.306	0	1
Limiting	.170	.377	0	1
Reluctant	.022	.148	0	1
Emphatic	.089	.286	0	1
No concurrence	.593	.493	0	1
Number of Dissents	1.156	.800	0	3
Age	6.056	4.871	0	16.167
Complexity	2.793	1.059	2	8
Political importance	.163	.371	0	1
Legal importance	.163	.371	0	1
Ideological incompatibility between Supreme Court and precedent	1.817	1.553	.001	5.114
Overruled	.052	.223	0	1
Positive Prior Net treatment by Supreme Court	.111	.870	−2	4

Notes

Chapter 1: Introduction

1. An attitudinalist believes that "the Supreme Court decides disputes in light of the facts of the case vis-à-vis the ideological attitudes and values of the justices" (Segal and Spaeth 1993, 65).

2. The U.S. legal system is based on the norm of *stare decisis*, a legal doctrine that encourages judges to follow precedent by letting the past decision stand (Black 1991, 978–79).

3. Students and staff were permitted to leave classes to watch the Olympic torch pass by.

4. In *Tinker*, students were suspended for wearing black armbands to school to demonstrate their opposition to the Vietnam War. The Court held that the students' First Amendment free speech rights were violated. Specifically, the Court held that state officials cannot suppress students' right to free speech unless school authorities reasonably believe school will be substantially disrupted or there will be "material interference with school activities" (514).

5. The First Amendment to the U.S. Constitution states, "Congress shall make no law respecting an establishment of religion." There is much debate about the meaning of the term *establishment of religion*. Some justices argue the term was intended to prohibit only the establishment of an official religion or preferring one religion rather than another. Others believe the term also prohibits the government from promoting religion in general.

6. The test derives its name from the case *Lemon v. Kurtzman* (1971), in which the Court struck down a state program providing aid to religious elementary and secondary schools.

7. When Roberts began his first term, he pushed the other justices toward narrow decisions in an effort to achieve more unanimous decisions. In conference, Roberts encouraged the justices to discuss the cases for a longer period of time than former Chief Justice Rehnquist had (Toobin 2007). And he indeed achieved a high level of consensus that first term. In fact, during Roberts' first term on the Court, 45 percent of the opinions were fully unanimous (no dissent or concurrence). However, during his second term, only 25 percent of the cases were fully unanimous and during his third term only 20 percent were fully unanimous.

8. Concurrences also can be categorized by whether they are regular or special concurrences. Regular concurrences accept both the majority opinion's result and its rationale while special concurrences endorse only the majority's result. Thus, a justice writing a regular concurrence is part of the majority voting coalition *and* the majority opinion coalition while the justice writing a special concurrence is only part of the majority voting coalition and is not considered part of the majority opinion coalition. Although these distinctions are very important, classifying concurrences on this basis does not explain the content of the concurrence and its full relationship to the majority opinion.

9. In *Miller v. California* (1973), the Court set out a three-part test for judging whether material is obscene. The third prong of the *Miller* test requires a determination of "whether the work, taken as a whole, lacks serious literary, artistic, political, or scientific value" (24).

Chapter 2: Why Justices Write or Join: Modeling Concurring Behavior

1. *Head & Armory v. Providence Ins. Co.* (1804).
2. *United States v. Fisher* (1805).
3. The data for the figure provided by Epstein, et al. (2007).
4. Values are from 1.00 (the most liberal) to −1.00 (the most conservative). The values were derived from content analyses of newspaper editorials prior to confirmation.
5. Maltzman, et al. (2000) used a different measure of cooperation, which is the residual from an ordinary least squares regression of ideology on the percentage of nonmajority opinions a justice joined with another justice in the previous term. According to Westerland (2004), there are two theoretical problems with that measure. First, it is very difficult to attach theoretical meaning to a measure that is a residual from a regression equation. The second problem is that the values are not dyadic. The justices have two different levels of cooperation for every term. Because the concept of cooperation is based on the favor being returned, it makes more sense to have dyadic values.
6. These are cases that (a) led to a story on the front page of *The New York Times* on the day after the Court handed down the decision; (b) were the lead cases in the story; and (c) were orally argued and decided with an opinion. A list of cases is contained in The Supreme Court Compendium (Epstein, et al. 2007).
7. In fact, in only eight cases was a doctrinal concurrence classified as a regular concurrence.
8. To note is to speak without opinion (Epstein and Knight 1998, 7).
9. I also excluded justices who only joined a concurring opinion in part.
10. If a justice both authored a concurring opinion and joined another, the justice is coded as having authored the opinion.

Chapter 3: Potential Concurrences: Insight from Justices Blackmun and Marshall

1. Two postulates form the basis of the collegial game: opinion authors pursue their policy preferences, but they do so within the strategic constraints imposed by their colleagues on the bench (Maltzman, et al. 2000).

2. The authors found that if the case is politically salient bargaining increases, while the chief justice is less likely to bargain with the majority opinion author. Finally, if the justice is an expert on an issue, he or she is more likely to bargain.

3. The authors found that if the case is politically salient or if the case is complex, the likelihood of an additional draft being circulated increases. Additionally, nonexperts are more likely to circulate additional draft opinions.

4. Justices occasionally circulate private memoranda to one or more colleagues, but not to the whole Court. I focused on the majority opinions written by Blackmun and Marshall in order to capture all of the bargaining and accommodation that occurred for a given opinion.

5. These are orally argued, signed opinions.

6. A bargaining statement is any memo (either from another justice or as indicated in one of Blackmun's clerk's memos) that a justice would like a change in the majority opinion.

7. Accommodation is a change by Blackmun in an attempt to address the justice's concern.

8. The Supremacy Clause of the Constitution states that the "Constitution and the laws of the United States . . . shall be the supreme law of the land . . . anything in the constitutions or laws of any State to the contrary notwithstanding." This means that any federal law trumps (or "preempts") any conflicting state law.

9. This memo was not circulated to the entire conference.

10. Brennan and Marshall.

11. According to *Hanna v. Plumer* (1965), when a federal rule and state law conflict, the *Hanna* analysis is relevant and the federal court is to apply the federal rule.

12. The Rules of Decisions Act requires that federal courts apply state law in their decisions, except when in conflict with federal law.

13. Powell, Brennan, and Blackmun.

14. In order for a court to issue an order to a person, it must have the authority to do so. This means the court must have personal jurisdiction over the person. For a court to have personal jurisdiction over a defendant, the defendant must have been personally served with process or the defendant must have some contacts with the state in which the court is located.

15. *Robertson v. Railroad Labor Board* (1925) held that a court lacks authority to issue process outside its district.

16. Attorney–client privilege is a legal concept that protects communications between a client and his attorney, keeping those communications confidential. However, if the client consults his attorney for advice in order to commit a crime or fraud, there is no privilege.

17. Fraud on the market theory is based on the hypothesis that, in an open and developed securities market, the price of a company's stock is determined by the available material information regarding the company and its business. Thus, misleading statements defraud purchasers of stock even if the purchasers do not directly rely on the misstatements.

18. Workers' compensation statutes generally contain "exclusivity" provisions that bar court suits for any bodily injury arising out of, and in the course of, employment (Holloway and Leech 2003).

19. An as-applied challenge means that the person is arguing: "This law is unconstitutional as applied to me." In contrast, a facial challenge means the person is arguing that the statute is always, under all circumstances, unconstitutional.

20. In this case, the Nevada statute provided that, in addition to a punishment of a minimum of two days and a maximum of six months imprisonment, the defendant also must pay a fine ranging from two-hundred to one-thousand dollars, and the defendant automatically loses his driver's license for ninety days and must attend an alcohol abuse education course.

21. The Court will not overturn a judgment on the basis of an error that was harmless. A harmless error is an insignificant error that does not change the outcome of the case.

22. The dismissal of jurors without stating the reason for dismissal.

23. In *Doe v. United States* (1988), a memo from Blackmun's clerk stated that Rehnquist's clerk called her and asked for two changes and that Rehnquist would join the opinion if they made those two changes. "I think we can and probably ought, since we are in need of a vote to clinch a majority" (Blackmun 1988g). Thus, the need for five votes can lead to accommodation. However, Blackmun accommodated other justices even when he already had a majority. In the same case, Scalia wrote Blackmun a memo, requesting changes. Blackmun modified the opinion to take into account some of Scalia's requests, even though he already had a Court.

24. *Batson v. Kentucky* (1986) was a case in which the Court held that a prosecutor's use of a peremptory challenge may not be used to exclude jurors based solely on their race.

25. Generally, the term *collateral review* refers to a proceeding separate and distinct from that in which the original judgment was rendered.

Chapter 4: The Impact of Concurring Opinions

1. More than thirty years later, the Court still uses the test articulated by Justice Harlan in his concurrence. For example, in *Kyllo v. U.S.* (2001), the Court applied the *Katz* test and found that the use of a thermal imaging device to scan Kyllo's home amounted to a Fourth Amendment "search" because it violated his "reasonable expectation of privacy."

2. Many appeals court panels include a district court judge. Although the Judicial Common Space scores are currently not available for district court judges, I calculated their scores using the same method.

3. Bonneau, Hammond, Maltzman, and Wahlbeck (2007) found substantial support for the agenda control model; thus, the use of the majority opinion writer's ideological position should be an appropriate proxy for the opinion policy's content.

4. Case importance operates on both a political and legal dimension (see Maltzman, et al. 2000). Thus, I use two measures of case importance.

5. These are cases that (a) led to a story on the front page of *The New York Times* on the day after the Court handed down the decision; (b) were the lead cases in the story; and (c) were orally argued and decided with an opinion.

6. To identify cases that have been overruled by the Supreme Court or overridden by Congress, I use *Shepard's* and the cases identified by Eskridge (1991).

7. I include all signed, orally argued Supreme Court opinions.

8. Although *Shepard's* does not capture whether lower courts ignore Supreme Court precedent as a means of noncompliance, evidence has been found to mitigate the seriousness of the problem for studying the Courts of Appeals. Specifically, Benesh and Reddick (2002) analyzed Courts of Appeals treatment of Supreme Court alterations of precedent. They identified common West Key numbers between the overruled and overruling decisions, ascertaining the issues that were the basis of the overruling. Then they obtained every lower court decision under those keys from the year of the overruling decision to 1999. Out of the thousands of cases generated, they examined a sample of those to determine if the lower courts were ignoring the change in precedent. They did not find a single opinion that overtly ignored an overruling decision. Thus, they concluded that, instead of disregarding precedent they disagreed with, the Courts of Appeals would find more subtle ways to avoid it.

9. If a citing case refers to a cited case but no treatment code is provided, this means the citing case contained a reference to but did not legally treat the cited case. This represents a nonsubstantive treatment of a cited case. Thus, I do not include all the cases that merely cited a Supreme Court precedent, because my focus is on positive versus negative treatment.

10. Spriggs and Hansford (2000) empirically tested the reliability of *Shepard's* analysis of Supreme Court opinions and assessed the validity of *Shepard's* treatment codes, finding them to be quite reliable and valid (see also Hansford and Spriggs 2006).

11. Prior to 1993, *Shepard's* used the "strongest letter rule" to determine which code to apply if two codes could be applied to the same point of law in the cited case (Spriggs and Hansford 2000). This rule arranged treatment codes in terms of strength. The order of strength was overruled, questioned, limited, criticized, followed, distinguished, explained, and harmonized. Beginning in 1993, *Shepard's* began giving multiple legal treatments to a cited case. In coding the cases used in this study, rather than have multiple legal treatments, I continue using *Shepard's* "strongest letter rule" to determine which code to apply. For example, if a citing case both distinguished and followed the precedent, I code the citing case as having followed the precedent.

12. For example, in *Griffith v. Kentucky* (1987) the Supreme Court held that new constitutional rules of criminal procedure are to be given retroactive effect in any case, state or federal, in which the conviction had not become final prior to the

announcement of the new rule. The First Circuit, in *United States v. Melvin* (1994) applied the retroactivity rule even though the new criminal procedure rule was not a constitutional rule. In contrast, the Third Circuit, in *Diggs v. Owens* (1987) declined to apply the retroactivity rule because the rule in question was a new procedural rule that was not constitutionally grounded. "[W]e hold that *Griffith* should be confined to constitutional rules of criminal procedure and thus does not require retroactive application of new procedural decisions not constitutionally grounded" (442) (The Third Circuit case was coded as distinguishing *Griffith*). Here, each circuit had a choice. They could expand the rule announced in *Griffith* to a different set of facts or they could confine the rule announced in *Griffith*. In either case, there is an argument that the panel was acting entirely reasonable. However, in the first case, the rule announced in *Griffith* is followed and thus, the Supreme Court precedent has made more of an impact, but in the second case, the Supreme Court precedent has been distinguished and thus the rule does not apply and has no impact on the case at all. The impact of the Supreme Court case, by not being applied to this set of facts, has been diminished.

13. There are two reasons for this exclusion. One is that, as stated earlier, my focus is on positive versus negative treatment of Supreme Court precedent. Additionally, as stated earlier, Spriggs and Hansford (2000) conducted a study to determine the reliability of *Shepard's*. They found that *Shepard's* coding of negative treatments and the followed code are reliable. Spriggs and Hansford also showed that the collapsed treatment codes (positive, negative, and neutral) were reliable; however, the neutral treatment category was the least reliable.

14. Twelve Supreme Court cases contained multiple concurrences, and a corresponding 217 Circuit Court cases interpreted those Supreme Court decisions. I address multiple concurrences in a later section of this chapter.

15. I also perform a logit regression using the number of concurrences instead of the types of concurrences as the independent variable. That analysis shows that the number of concurrences is not statistically significant. This underscores the importance of categorizing the concurrences into different types in order to ascertain the true impact they have on lower court compliance.

16. Additionally, the baseline probability is based on the assumption that the Supreme Court case is not politically or legally important, has not been overruled, and is being treated by the Ninth Circuit. In the appendix, I provide predicted probabilities of positive treatment for each circuit.

17. This does not mean that the reason the lower court is limiting, distinguishing, questioning, or criticizing the case is not legitimate. In fact, Benesh (2002) found that when the Courts of Appeals do avoid applying a Supreme Court precedent, they justify their decisions by citing moderately persuasive reasons.

18. I include all signed, orally argued Supreme Court opinions.

19. There are two reasons for this exclusion. One is that, as stated earlier, my focus is on positive versus negative treatment of Supreme Court precedent. Additionally, as stated earlier, Spriggs and Hansford (2000) conducted a study to determine the reliability of *Shepard's*. They found that *Shepard's* coding of negative treatments and the followed code are reliable. Spriggs and Hansford also showed that the collapsed

treatment codes (positive, negative, and neutral) were reliable; however, the neutral treatment category was the least reliable.

20. The category of unnecessary concurrence predicts failure perfectly so it is dropped and two observations are not used.

References

Baird, Vanessa A. 2007. *Answering the call of the court: how justices and litigants set the Supreme Court agenda.* Charlottesville: University of Virginia Press.

Baum, Lawrence. 1978. Lower court response to Supreme Court decisions: Reconsidering a negative picture. *Justice System Journal* 3: 208–19.

———. 2007. *The Supreme Court.* 9th ed. Washington DC: Congressional Quarterly Press.

Benesh, Sara C. 2002. *The U.S. Court of Appeals and the law of confessions.* New York: LFB Scholarly Publishing LLC.

——— and Malia Reddick. 2002. Overruled: An event history analysis of lower court reaction to Supreme Court alteration of precedent. *The Journal of Politics* 64(2): 534–50.

——— and Harold J. Spaeth. 2003. *Justice-centered Rehnquist Court database, 1986–2000 terms.* Ann Arbor, MI: Inter-University Consortium for Political and Social Research.

Berkolow. 2008. Much ado about pluralities: Pride and precedent amidst the cacophony of concurrences, and re-Percolation after *Rapanos. Virginia Journal of Social Policy and the Law* 15: 299–354.

Black, Henry Campbell. 1991. *Black's law dictionary.* St. Paul, MN: West Publishing Company.

Blackmun, Harry A. 1986a. Memo from Antonin Scalia to Harry Blackmun, Nov. 25. Papers of Harry A. Blackmun. Washington, DC: Library of Congress Manuscript Division.

———. 1986b. Memo from law clerk to Harry Blackmun, Nov. 25. Papers of Harry A. Blackmun. Washington, DC: Library of Congress Manuscript Division.

———. 1986c. Memo from Harry Blackmun to John Paul Stevens and Sandra Day O'Connor, Nov. 26. Papers of Harry A. Blackmun. Washington, DC: Library of Congress Manuscript Division.

———. 1986d. Memo from Sandra Day O'Connor to Harry Blackmun, Nov. 28. Papers of Harry A. Blackmun. Washington, DC: Library of Congress Manuscript Division.

———. 1986e. Memo from Harry Blackmun to John Paul Stevens, Dec. 1. Papers of Harry A. Blackmun. Washington, DC: Library of Congress Manuscript Division.

———. 1986f. Memo from Antonin Scalia to Harry Blackmun, Dec. 1. Papers of Harry A. Blackmun. Washington, DC: Library of Congress Manuscript Division.

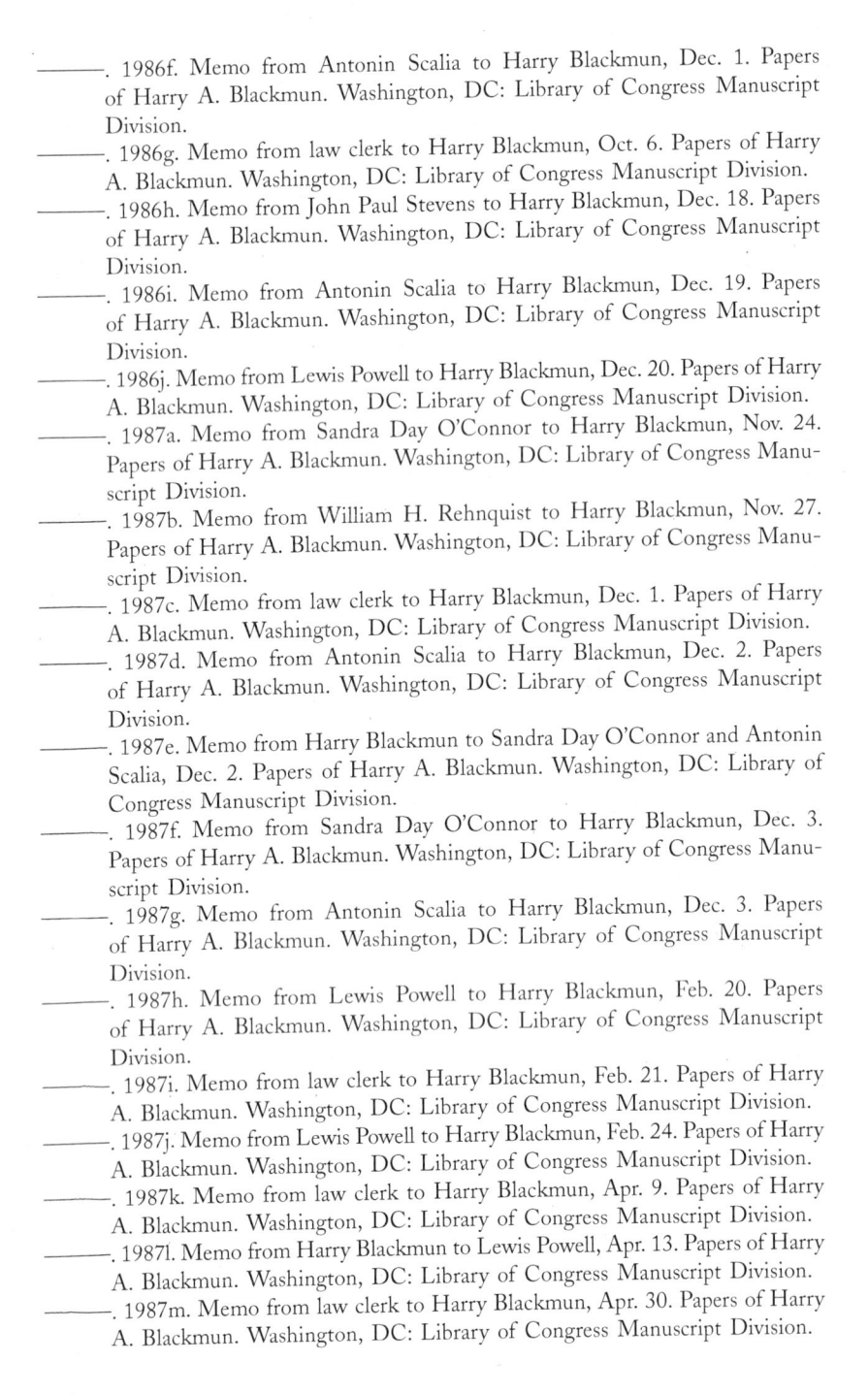

———. 1986g. Memo from law clerk to Harry Blackmun, Oct. 6. Papers of Harry A. Blackmun. Washington, DC: Library of Congress Manuscript Division.

———. 1986h. Memo from John Paul Stevens to Harry Blackmun, Dec. 18. Papers of Harry A. Blackmun. Washington, DC: Library of Congress Manuscript Division.

———. 1986i. Memo from Antonin Scalia to Harry Blackmun, Dec. 19. Papers of Harry A. Blackmun. Washington, DC: Library of Congress Manuscript Division.

———. 1986j. Memo from Lewis Powell to Harry Blackmun, Dec. 20. Papers of Harry A. Blackmun. Washington, DC: Library of Congress Manuscript Division.

———. 1987a. Memo from Sandra Day O'Connor to Harry Blackmun, Nov. 24. Papers of Harry A. Blackmun. Washington, DC: Library of Congress Manuscript Division.

———. 1987b. Memo from William H. Rehnquist to Harry Blackmun, Nov. 27. Papers of Harry A. Blackmun. Washington, DC: Library of Congress Manuscript Division.

———. 1987c. Memo from law clerk to Harry Blackmun, Dec. 1. Papers of Harry A. Blackmun. Washington, DC: Library of Congress Manuscript Division.

———. 1987d. Memo from Antonin Scalia to Harry Blackmun, Dec. 2. Papers of Harry A. Blackmun. Washington, DC: Library of Congress Manuscript Division.

———. 1987e. Memo from Harry Blackmun to Sandra Day O'Connor and Antonin Scalia, Dec. 2. Papers of Harry A. Blackmun. Washington, DC: Library of Congress Manuscript Division.

———. 1987f. Memo from Sandra Day O'Connor to Harry Blackmun, Dec. 3. Papers of Harry A. Blackmun. Washington, DC: Library of Congress Manuscript Division.

———. 1987g. Memo from Antonin Scalia to Harry Blackmun, Dec. 3. Papers of Harry A. Blackmun. Washington, DC: Library of Congress Manuscript Division.

———. 1987h. Memo from Lewis Powell to Harry Blackmun, Feb. 20. Papers of Harry A. Blackmun. Washington, DC: Library of Congress Manuscript Division.

———. 1987i. Memo from law clerk to Harry Blackmun, Feb. 21. Papers of Harry A. Blackmun. Washington, DC: Library of Congress Manuscript Division.

———. 1987j. Memo from Lewis Powell to Harry Blackmun, Feb. 24. Papers of Harry A. Blackmun. Washington, DC: Library of Congress Manuscript Division.

———. 1987k. Memo from law clerk to Harry Blackmun, Apr. 9. Papers of Harry A. Blackmun. Washington, DC: Library of Congress Manuscript Division.

———. 1987l. Memo from Harry Blackmun to Lewis Powell, Apr. 13. Papers of Harry A. Blackmun. Washington, DC: Library of Congress Manuscript Division.

———. 1987m. Memo from law clerk to Harry Blackmun, Apr. 30. Papers of Harry A. Blackmun. Washington, DC: Library of Congress Manuscript Division.

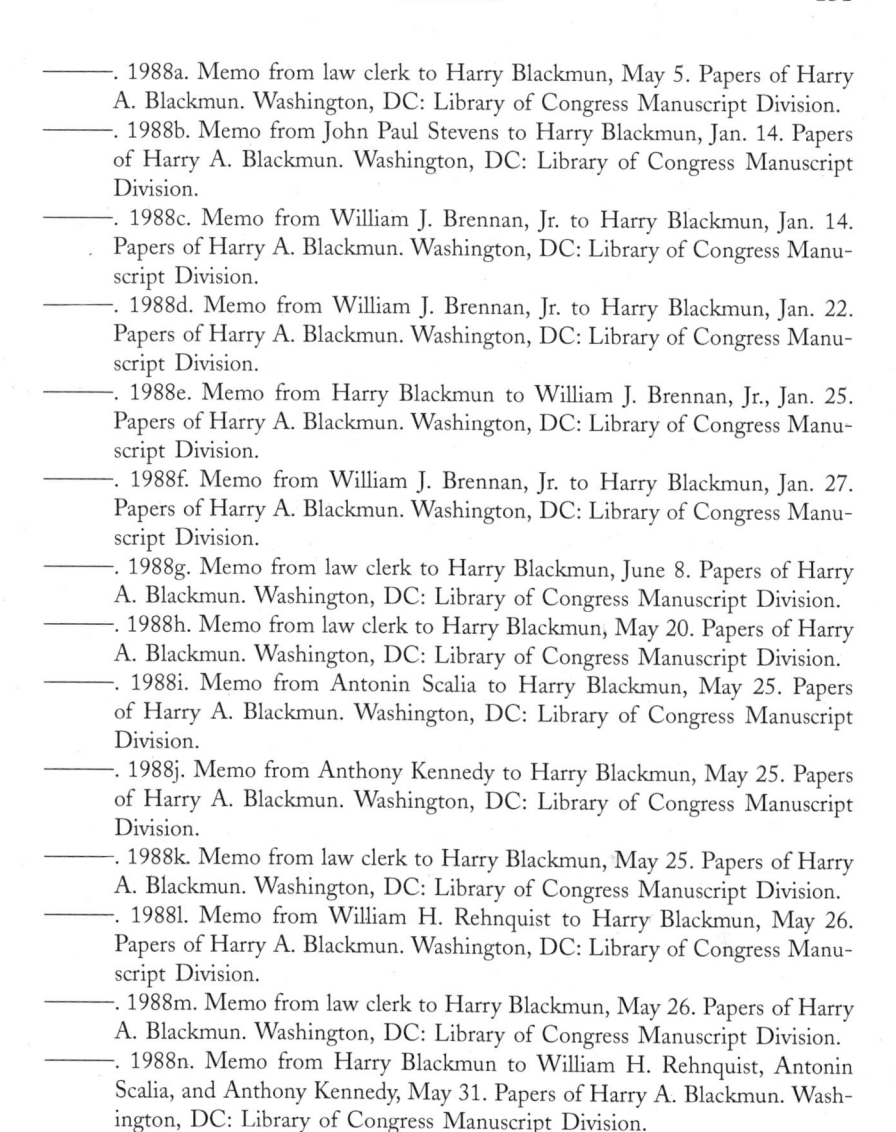

―――. 1988a. Memo from law clerk to Harry Blackmun, May 5. Papers of Harry A. Blackmun. Washington, DC: Library of Congress Manuscript Division.

―――. 1988b. Memo from John Paul Stevens to Harry Blackmun, Jan. 14. Papers of Harry A. Blackmun. Washington, DC: Library of Congress Manuscript Division.

―――. 1988c. Memo from William J. Brennan, Jr. to Harry Blackmun, Jan. 14. Papers of Harry A. Blackmun. Washington, DC: Library of Congress Manuscript Division.

―――. 1988d. Memo from William J. Brennan, Jr. to Harry Blackmun, Jan. 22. Papers of Harry A. Blackmun. Washington, DC: Library of Congress Manuscript Division.

―――. 1988e. Memo from Harry Blackmun to William J. Brennan, Jr., Jan. 25. Papers of Harry A. Blackmun. Washington, DC: Library of Congress Manuscript Division.

―――. 1988f. Memo from William J. Brennan, Jr. to Harry Blackmun, Jan. 27. Papers of Harry A. Blackmun. Washington, DC: Library of Congress Manuscript Division.

―――. 1988g. Memo from law clerk to Harry Blackmun, June 8. Papers of Harry A. Blackmun. Washington, DC: Library of Congress Manuscript Division.

―――. 1988h. Memo from law clerk to Harry Blackmun, May 20. Papers of Harry A. Blackmun. Washington, DC: Library of Congress Manuscript Division.

―――. 1988i. Memo from Antonin Scalia to Harry Blackmun, May 25. Papers of Harry A. Blackmun. Washington, DC: Library of Congress Manuscript Division.

―――. 1988j. Memo from Anthony Kennedy to Harry Blackmun, May 25. Papers of Harry A. Blackmun. Washington, DC: Library of Congress Manuscript Division.

―――. 1988k. Memo from law clerk to Harry Blackmun, May 25. Papers of Harry A. Blackmun. Washington, DC: Library of Congress Manuscript Division.

―――. 1988l. Memo from William H. Rehnquist to Harry Blackmun, May 26. Papers of Harry A. Blackmun. Washington, DC: Library of Congress Manuscript Division.

―――. 1988m. Memo from law clerk to Harry Blackmun, May 26. Papers of Harry A. Blackmun. Washington, DC: Library of Congress Manuscript Division.

―――. 1988n. Memo from Harry Blackmun to William H. Rehnquist, Antonin Scalia, and Anthony Kennedy, May 31. Papers of Harry A. Blackmun. Washington, DC: Library of Congress Manuscript Division.

―――. 1989a. Memo from William H. Rehnquist to Harry Blackmun, Mar. 27. Papers of Harry A. Blackmun. Washington, DC: Library of Congress Manuscript Division.

―――. 1989b. Memo from Anthony Kennedy to Harry Blackmun, June 9. Papers of Harry A. Blackmun. Washington, DC: Library of Congress Manuscript Division.

―――. 1989c. Memo from Harry Blackmun to Anthony Kennedy, June 9. Papers of Harry A. Blackmun. Washington, DC: Library of Congress Manuscript Division.

———. 1989d. Memo from Antonin Scalia to Harry Blackmun, June 14. Papers of Harry A. Blackmun. Washington, DC: Library of Congress Manuscript Division.

———. 1989e. Memo from Harry Blackmun to Antonin Scalia, June 14. Papers of Harry A. Blackmun. Washington, DC: Library of Congress Manuscript Division.

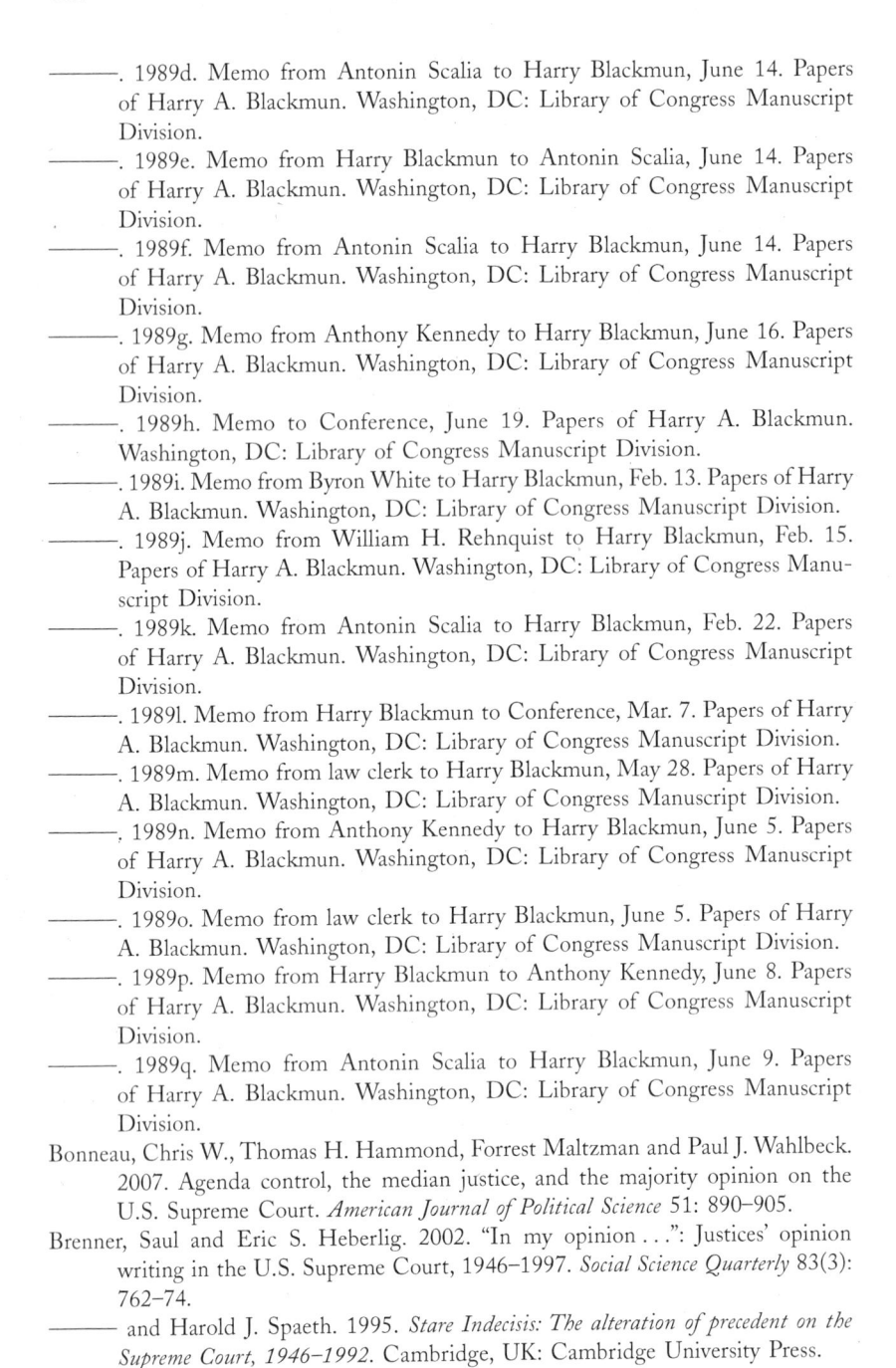

———. 1989f. Memo from Antonin Scalia to Harry Blackmun, June 14. Papers of Harry A. Blackmun. Washington, DC: Library of Congress Manuscript Division.

———. 1989g. Memo from Anthony Kennedy to Harry Blackmun, June 16. Papers of Harry A. Blackmun. Washington, DC: Library of Congress Manuscript Division.

———. 1989h. Memo to Conference, June 19. Papers of Harry A. Blackmun. Washington, DC: Library of Congress Manuscript Division.

———. 1989i. Memo from Byron White to Harry Blackmun, Feb. 13. Papers of Harry A. Blackmun. Washington, DC: Library of Congress Manuscript Division.

———. 1989j. Memo from William H. Rehnquist to Harry Blackmun, Feb. 15. Papers of Harry A. Blackmun. Washington, DC: Library of Congress Manuscript Division.

———. 1989k. Memo from Antonin Scalia to Harry Blackmun, Feb. 22. Papers of Harry A. Blackmun. Washington, DC: Library of Congress Manuscript Division.

———. 1989l. Memo from Harry Blackmun to Conference, Mar. 7. Papers of Harry A. Blackmun. Washington, DC: Library of Congress Manuscript Division.

———. 1989m. Memo from law clerk to Harry Blackmun, May 28. Papers of Harry A. Blackmun. Washington, DC: Library of Congress Manuscript Division.

———. 1989n. Memo from Anthony Kennedy to Harry Blackmun, June 5. Papers of Harry A. Blackmun. Washington, DC: Library of Congress Manuscript Division.

———. 1989o. Memo from law clerk to Harry Blackmun, June 5. Papers of Harry A. Blackmun. Washington, DC: Library of Congress Manuscript Division.

———. 1989p. Memo from Harry Blackmun to Anthony Kennedy, June 8. Papers of Harry A. Blackmun. Washington, DC: Library of Congress Manuscript Division.

———. 1989q. Memo from Antonin Scalia to Harry Blackmun, June 9. Papers of Harry A. Blackmun. Washington, DC: Library of Congress Manuscript Division.

Bonneau, Chris W., Thomas H. Hammond, Forrest Maltzman and Paul J. Wahlbeck. 2007. Agenda control, the median justice, and the majority opinion on the U.S. Supreme Court. *American Journal of Political Science* 51: 890–905.

Brenner, Saul and Eric S. Heberlig. 2002. "In my opinion...": Justices' opinion writing in the U.S. Supreme Court, 1946–1997. *Social Science Quarterly* 83(3): 762–74.

——— and Harold J. Spaeth. 1995. *Stare Indecisis: The alteration of precedent on the Supreme Court, 1946–1992*. Cambridge, UK: Cambridge University Press.

References

Brent, James C. 1999. An agent and two principals: U.S. Court of Appeals responses to *Employment Division, Department of Human Resources v. Smith* and the Religious Freedom Restoration Act. *American Politics Quarterly* 27(2): 236–66.

Caldeira, Gregory A. and Christopher J.W. Zorn. 1998.Of time and consensual norms in the Supreme Court. *American Journal of Political Science* 42: 874–902.

Caminker, Evan H. 1994. Why must inferior courts obey Superior precedents? *Stanford Law Review* 46: 817–73.

Canon, Bradley C. 1973. Reactions of state Supreme Courts to a U.S. Supreme Court civil liberties decision. *Law and Society Review* 8: 109–34.

―――― and Charles Johnson. 1999. *Judicial policies: implementation and impact.* 2nd ed. Washington, DC: Congressional Quarterly Press.

Collins, Paul. 2004. Variable voting behavior on the Supreme Court: A preliminary analysis and research framework. *Justice System Journal* 25: 57–74.

Corley, Pamela C. 2009. Uncertain precedent: Circuit Court responses to Supreme Court plurality opinions." *American Politics Research* 37: 30–49.

Epstein, Lee and Jack Knight. 1998. *The choices justices make.* Washington, DC: Congressional Quarterly Press.

―――― and Joseph F. Kobylka. 1992. *The Supreme Court and legal change: abortion and the death penalty.* Chapel Hill: University of North Carolina Press.

――――, Andrew D. Martin, Jeffrey A. Segal, and Chad Westerland. 2007. The judicial common space. *Journal of Law, Economics, and Organization* 23: 303–25.

―――― and Jeffrey A. Segal. 2000. Measuring issue salience. *American Journal of Political Science* 44: 66–83.

――――, Jeffrey A. Segal, Harold J. Spaeth, and Thomas G. Walker. 2007. *The Supreme Court Compendium: data, decisions, and developments.* 4th ed. Washington, DC: Congressional Quarterly Press.

Eskridge, William N. Jr. 1991. Overriding Supreme Court statutory interpretation decisions. *Yale Law Journal* 101: 331–417.

Fuld, Stanley H. 1962.The voices of dissent. *Columbia Law Review* 62: 923–29.

Ginsburg, Ruth Bader. 1990. Remarks on writing separately. *Washington Law Review* 65: 133–50.

Greenburg, Jan Crawford. 2007. *Supreme conflict: the inside story of the struggle for control of the United States Supreme Court.* New York: The Penguin Press.

Gruhl, John. 1980. The Supreme Court's impact on the law of libel: compliance by lower federal courts. *Western Political Quarterly* 33: 503–19.

Hall, Melinda Gann and Paul Brace. 1992. Toward an integrated model of judicial voting behavior. *American Politics Quarterly* 20: 147–68.

Hansford, Thomas G. and James F. Spriggs II. 2006. *The politics of precedent on the U.S. Supreme Court.* Princeton, NJ: Princeton University Press.

Haynie, Stacia L. 1992. Leadership and consensus on the U.S. Supreme Court. *Journal of Politics* 54: 1158–169.

Hettinger, Virginia A., Stefanie A. Lindquist, and Wendy L. Martinek. 2003. Acclimation Effects and separate opinion writing in the U.S. Courts of Appeals. *Social Science Quarterly* 84(4): 792–810.

———, Stefanie A. Lindquist, and Wendy L. Martinek. 2006. *Judging on a collegial court: influences on federal appellate decision making.* Charlottesville: University of Virginia Press.

Holloway, William J. and Michael J. Leech. 2003. *Employment termination: rights and remedies.* 2nd ed. Washington, DC: BNA Books.

Johnson, Charles A. 1979. Lower Court reactions to Supreme Court decisions: A quantitative examination. *American Journal of Political Science* 23(4): 792–804.

———. 1987. Law, politics, and judicial decision making: Lower federal court uses of Supreme Court decisions. *Law and Society Review* 21: 325–39.

Klein, David E. 2002. *Making law in the United States Courts of Appeals.* New York: Cambridge University Press.

Kluger, Richard. 1977. *Simple justice.* New York: Vintage Books.

Kolsky, Meredith. 1995. Justice William Johnson and the history of the Supreme Court dissent. *Georgetown Law Journal* 83: 2069–98.

Lazarus, Edward P. 1998. *Closed chambers: The first eyewitness account of the epic struggles inside the Supreme Court.* New York: Random House.

Levinson, Sanford. 2000. Why the Canon should be expanded to include the insular cases and the saga of American expansionism. *Constitutional Commentary* 17: 241–66.

Long, J. Scott and Jeremy Freese. 2001. *Regression models for categorical dependent variables using stata.* College Station, TX: A Stata Press Publication.

Maltzman, Forrest, James F. Spriggs II, and Paul J. Wahlbeck. 2000. *Crafting law on the Supreme Court: the collegial game.* New York: Cambridge University Press.

Marshall, Thurgood. 1987a. Memo from law clerk to Thurgood Marshall. Papers of Thurgood Marshall. Washington, DC: Library of Congress Manuscript Division.

———. 1987b. Memo from William J. Brennan, Jr. to Thurgood Marshall, January 9. Papers of Thurgood Marshall. Washington, DC: Library of Congress Manuscript Division.

———. 1987c. Memo from Lewis Powell to Thurgood Marshall, January 15. Papers of Thurgood Marshall. Washington, DC: Library of Congress Manuscript Division.

———. 1987d. Memo from William J. Brennan, Jr. to Thurgood Marshall, January 16. Papers of Thurgood Marshall. Washington, DC: Library of Congress Manuscript Division.

———. 1987e. Memo from law clerk to Thurgood Marshall, January 16. Papers of Thurgood Marshall. Washington, DC: Library of Congress Manuscript Division.

———. 1987f. Memo from Thurgood Marshall to William J. Brennan, Jr. and Lewis Powell, January 16. Papers of Thurgood Marshall. Washington, DC: Library of Congress Manuscript Division.

———. 1987g. Memo from John Paul Stevens to Thurgood Marshall, November 9. Papers of Thurgood Marshall. Washington, DC: Library of Congress Manuscript Division.

References

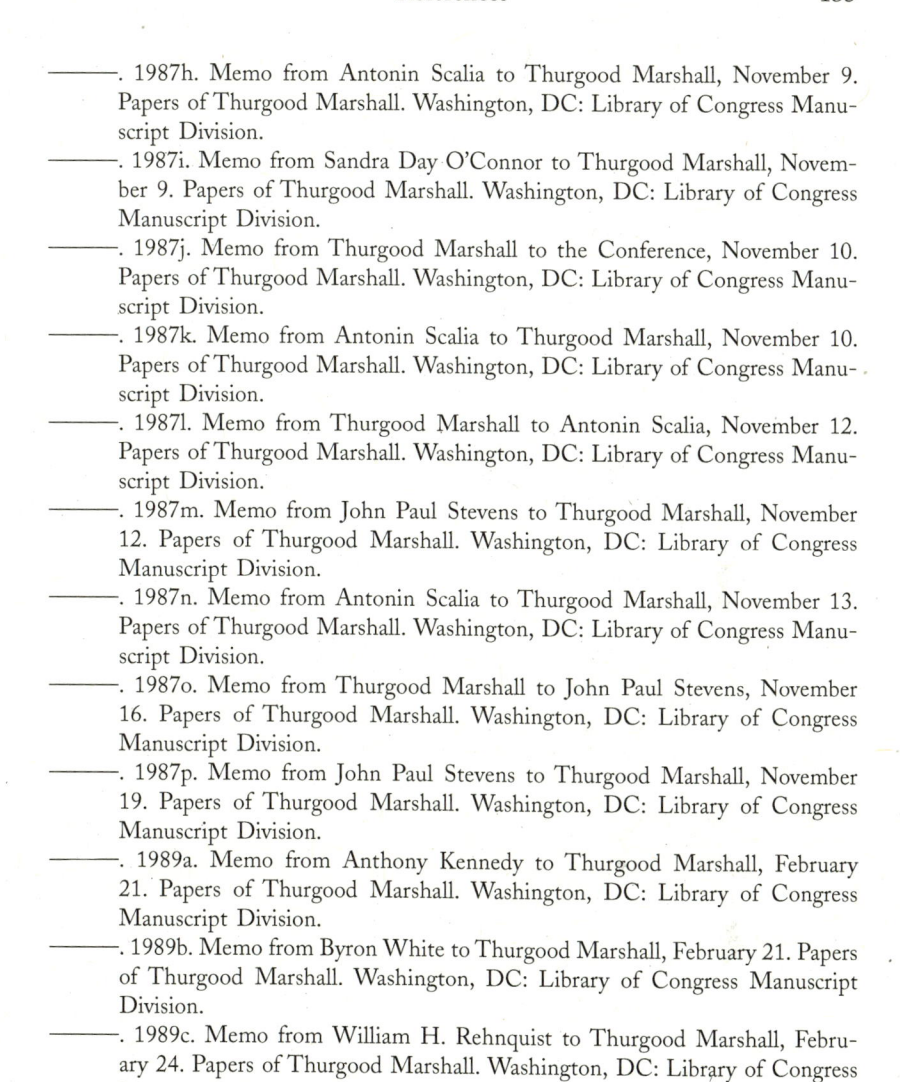

———. 1987h. Memo from Antonin Scalia to Thurgood Marshall, November 9. Papers of Thurgood Marshall. Washington, DC: Library of Congress Manuscript Division.

———. 1987i. Memo from Sandra Day O'Connor to Thurgood Marshall, November 9. Papers of Thurgood Marshall. Washington, DC: Library of Congress Manuscript Division.

———. 1987j. Memo from Thurgood Marshall to the Conference, November 10. Papers of Thurgood Marshall. Washington, DC: Library of Congress Manuscript Division.

———. 1987k. Memo from Antonin Scalia to Thurgood Marshall, November 10. Papers of Thurgood Marshall. Washington, DC: Library of Congress Manuscript Division.

———. 1987l. Memo from Thurgood Marshall to Antonin Scalia, November 12. Papers of Thurgood Marshall. Washington, DC: Library of Congress Manuscript Division.

———. 1987m. Memo from John Paul Stevens to Thurgood Marshall, November 12. Papers of Thurgood Marshall. Washington, DC: Library of Congress Manuscript Division.

———. 1987n. Memo from Antonin Scalia to Thurgood Marshall, November 13. Papers of Thurgood Marshall. Washington, DC: Library of Congress Manuscript Division.

———. 1987o. Memo from Thurgood Marshall to John Paul Stevens, November 16. Papers of Thurgood Marshall. Washington, DC: Library of Congress Manuscript Division.

———. 1987p. Memo from John Paul Stevens to Thurgood Marshall, November 19. Papers of Thurgood Marshall. Washington, DC: Library of Congress Manuscript Division.

———. 1989a. Memo from Anthony Kennedy to Thurgood Marshall, February 21. Papers of Thurgood Marshall. Washington, DC: Library of Congress Manuscript Division.

———. 1989b. Memo from Byron White to Thurgood Marshall, February 21. Papers of Thurgood Marshall. Washington, DC: Library of Congress Manuscript Division.

———. 1989c. Memo from William H. Rehnquist to Thurgood Marshall, February 24. Papers of Thurgood Marshall. Washington, DC: Library of Congress Manuscript Division.

———. 1989d. Memo from Thurgood Marshall to William H. Rehnquist, Byron White, and Anthony Kennedy, February 28. Papers of Thurgood Marshall. Washington, DC: Library of Congress Manuscript Division.

———. 1989e. Memo from Anthony Kennedy to Thurgood Marshall, March 1. Papers of Thurgood Marshall. Washington, DC: Library of Congress Manuscript Division.

———. 1990a. Memo from Sandra Day O'Connor to Thurgood Marshall, February 15. Papers of Thurgood Marshall. Washington, DC: Library of Congress Manuscript Division.

———. 1990b. Memo from Antonin Scalia to Thurgood Marshall, February 15. Papers of Thurgood Marshall. Washington, DC: Library of Congress Manuscript Division.

———. 1990c. Memo from Byron White to Thurgood Marshall, February 16. Papers of Thurgood Marshall. Washington, DC: Library of Congress Manuscript Division.

———. 1990d. Memo from Anthony Kennedy to Thurgood Marshall, February 20. Papers of Thurgood Marshall. Washington, DC: Library of Congress Manuscript Division.

———. 1990e. Memo from William H. Rehnquist to Thurgood Marshall, February 22. Papers of Thurgood Marshall. Washington, DC: Library of Congress Manuscript Division.

———. 1990f. Memo from Sandra Day O'Connor to Thurgood Marshall, February 28. Papers of Thurgood Marshall. Washington, DC: Library of Congress Manuscript Division.

Maveety, Nancy. 2002. *Concurrence and the study of judicial behavior*. Paper presented at the annual meeting of the American Political Science Association, Boston.

———. 2003. *Concurring opinion writing and the bifurcation of judicial goals*. Paper presented at the annual meeting of the American Political Science Association, Philadelphia.

———. 2005. The era of the Choral Court. *Judicature* 89: 138–45.

Mendelson, Wallace. 1963. The neo-behavioral approach to the judicial process: A critique. *American Political Science Review* 57: 593–603.

Moorhead, R. Dean. 1952. Concurring and dissenting opinions. *American Bar Association Journal* 38: 821–24.

Murphy, Walter F. 1964. *Elements of judicial strategy*. Chicago: University of Chicago Press.

O'Brien, David M. 1999. Institutional norms and Supreme Court opinions: on reconsidering the rise of individual opinions. In *Supreme Court decision-making: new institutionalist approaches*, eds. Cornell W. Clayton and Howard Gillman. Chicago: Chicago University Press.

Pacelle, Richard L., Jr. 1991. *The transformation of the Court's agenda: from the New Deal to the Reagan Administration*. Boulder, CO: Westview Press.

Paulsen, Michael Stokes. 2002. Youngstown goes to war. *Constitutional Commentary* 19: 215–59.

Perry, H. W., Jr. 1991. *Deciding to decide: agenda setting in the United States Supreme Court*. Cambridge, MA: Harvard University Press.

Phillips, Harlan B. 1960. *Felix Frankfurter reminisces*. New York: Reynal.

Pritchett, C. Herman. 1948. *The Roosevelt Court: a study in judicial politics and values, 1937–1947*. New York: Macmillan.

Ray, Laura Krugman. 1990. The justices write separately: uses of the concurrence by the Rehnquist Court. *University of California, Davis Law Review* 23: 777–831.

Rehnquist, William H. 1992. Remarks on the process of judging. *Washington and Lee Law Review* 49: 263–70.

Rohde, David and Harold Spaeth. 1976. *Supreme Court decision making*. San Francisco: W.H. Freeman.

Rosen, Jeffrey. 2006. *The Supreme Court: the personalities and rivalries that defined America*. New York: Times Books.

Scalia, Antonin. 1994. The dissenting opinion. *Journal of Supreme Court History* 33–44.

Schubert, Glendon. 1959. *Quantitative analysis of judicial behavior*. Glencoe, IL: The Free Press.

———. 1965. *The judicial mind:the attitudes and ideologies of Supreme Court justices, 1946–1963*. Evanston, IL: Northwestern University Press.

Schwartz, Bernard. 1957. *The Supreme Court: constitutional revolution in retrospect*. New York: The Ronald Press Co.

———. 1996. *Decision: how the Supreme Court decides cases*. New York: Oxford University Press.

Segal, Jeffrey A. and Albert D. Cover. 1989. Ideological values and the votes of the U.S. Supreme Court justices. *American Political Science Review* 83: 557–65.

——— and Harold J. Spaeth. 1993. *The Supreme Court and the attitudinal model*. New York: Cambridge University Press.

——— and Harold J. Spaeth. 2002. *The Supreme Court and the attitudinal model revisited*. New York: Cambridge University Press.

——— and Harold J. Spaeth. 2003. Reply to the critics of the Supreme Court attitudinal model revisited. *Law and Courts* (Summer): 31–38.

Songer, Donald, and Susan Haire. 1992. Integrating alterative approaches to the study of judicial voting: obscenity cases in the U.S. Courts of Appeals. *American Journal of Political Science* 36: 963–82.

——— and Reginald S. Sheehan. 1990. Supreme Court impact on compliance and outcomes: Miranda and New York Times in the United States Courts of Appeals. *Western Political Quarterly* 43: 297–316.

Spaeth, Harold J. 1965. Jurimetrics and professor Mendelson: a troubled relationship. *Journal of Politics* 27: 875–80.

———. 1995. "The Attitudinal Model." In *Contemplating Courts*, ed. Lee Epstein, 296–314. Washington, DC: CQ Press.

———. 2007. *The United States Supreme Court Judicial Database, 1953–2006 terms*. East Lansing: Michigan State University, Department of Political Science (producer); Lexington: S. Sidney Ulmer Project for Research in Law and Judicial Politics, Department of Political Science, University of Kentucky (distributor).

Specter, Arlen. 2006. Transcript of U.S. Senate Judiciary Committee hearing on Judge Samuel Alito's nomination to the Supreme Court. *Washington Post*. http://www.washingtonpost.com/wp-dyn/content/article/2006/01/09/AR200601090755.html. Accessed January 9, 2009.

Spriggs, James F., II. 2003. The attitudinal model: an explanation of case dispositions, not substantive policy outcomes. *Law and Courts* (Summer): 10–38.

——— and Thomas G. Hansford. 2000. Measuring legal change: the reliability and validity of *Shepard's Citations*. *Political Research Quarterly* 53(2): 327–41.

——— and Thomas G. Hansford. 2001. Explaining the overruling of U.S. Supreme Court precedent. *The Journal of Politics* 63(4): 1091–111.

Tarr, G.A. 1977. *Judicial impact of the United States courts*. Lexington, MA: Lexington Books.

Toobin, Jeffrey. 2007. *The nine: inside the secret world of the Supreme Court.* New York: Doubleday.

Turner, Charles C. and Lori Beth Way. 2003. *Writing for the future: the dynamics of Supreme Court concurrence.* Paper presented at the annual meeting of the American Political Science Association, Philadelphia.

Ulmer, S. Sidney. 1959. An empirical analysis of selected aspects of lawmaking in the United States Supreme Court. *Journal of Public Law* 8: 414–36.

Wahlbeck, Paul J. 1997. "The Life of the Law: Judicial Politics and Legal Change." *Journal of Politics* 59: 778–802.

———, James F. Spriggs II, and Forrest Maltzman. 1998. Marshaling the court: bargaining and accommodation on the United States Supreme Court. *American Journal of Political Science* 42(1): 294–315.

———, James F. Spriggs II, and Forrest Maltzman. 1999. The politics of dissents and concurrences on the U.S. Supreme Court. *American Politics Quarterly* 27(4): 488–514.

Walker, Thomas G., Lee Epstein, and William J. Dixon. 1988. On the mysterious demise of consensual norms in the United States Supreme Court. *The Journal of Politics* 50: 361–89.

Ward, Artemus and David L. Weiden. 2006. *Sorcerers' apprentices: 100 years of law clerks at the United States Supreme Court.* New York: New York University Press.

Warren, Earl. 1977. *The memoirs of Chief Justice Warren.* Garden City, NY: Doubleday.

Wasby, Stephen. 1970. *The impact of the United States Supreme Court: some perspectives.* Homewood, IL: The Dorsey Press.

Way, Lori Beth and Charles C. Turner. 2006. Disagreement on the Rehnquist Court: the dynamics of Supreme Court concurrence." *American Politics Research* 34: 292–318.

Westerland, Chad. 2004. *Cooperative norms on the U.S. Supreme Court.* Paper presented at the annual meeting of the American Political Science Association, Chicago.

Witkin, B.E. 1977. *Manual on Appellate Court opinions.* St. Paul, MN: West Publishing Company.

Woodward, Bob, and Scott Armstrong. 1979. *The brethren: inside the Supreme Court.* New York: Simon and Schuster.

Table of Cases

Adams Fruit Co. v. Barrett. 1990. 494 U.S. 638.
Adams v. Texas, 1980. 448 U.S. 38.
Basic v. Levinson. 1988. 485 U.S. 224.
Batson v. Kentucky. 1986. 476 U.S. 79.
Blanton v. North Las Vegas. 1989. 489 U.S. 538.
Brown v. Board of Education. 1954. 347 U.S. 483.
Burlington Northern v. Woods. 1987. 480 U.S. 1.
Celotex Corp. v. Catrett. 1986. 477 U.S. 317.
Clarke v. Securities Industry Ass'n. 1987. 479 U.S. 388.
Colorado v. Connelly. 1986. 479 U.S. 157.
Connecticut v. Barrett. 1987. 479 U.S. 523.
County of Allegheny v. ACLU. 1989. 492 U.S. 573.
Coy v. Iowa. 1988. 487 U.S. 1012.
Dames & Moore v. Regan. 1981. 453 U.S. 654.
Davis v. Georgia. 1976. 429 U.S. 122.
Diggs v. Owens. 1987. 833 F.2d 439.
Doe. v. United States. 1988. 487 U.S. 201.
F.C.C. v. Florida Power Co. 1987. 480 U.S. 245.
Gray v. Mississippi. 1987. 481 U.S. 648.
Griffith v. Kentucky. 1987. 479 U.S. 314.
Gwaltney v. Chesapeake Bay Foundation. 1987. 484 U.S. 49.
Hankerson v. North Carolina, 1977. 432 U.S. 233.
Hanna v. Plumer. 1965. 380 U.S. 460.
Head & Armory v. Providence Ins. Co. 1804. 6 U.S. (2 Cranch) 127.
INS v. Cardoza-Fonseca. 1987. 480 U.S. 421.
Katz v. U.S. 1967. 389 U.S. 347.
Kentucky Dept. of Corrections v. Thompson. 1989. 490 U.S. 454.
Kyllo v. U.S. 2001. 533 U.S. 27.
Lemon v. Kurtzman. 1971. 403 U.S. 602.
Lynch v. Donnelly. 1984. 465 U.S. 668.
Mackey v. United States. 1971. 401 U.S. 667.

Marks v. U.S. 1977. 430 U.S. 188.
Maryland v. Craig. 1990. 497 U.S. 836.
Mathews v. U.S. 1988. 485 U.S. 58.
Michigan v. Chesternut. 1988. 486 U.S. 567.
Miller v. California. 1973. 413 U.S. 15.
Morse v. Frederick. 2007. 127 S. Ct. 2618.
Omni v. Wolff. 1987. 484 U.S. 97.
Pinter v. Dahl. 1988. 486 U.S. 622.
Pope v. Illinois. 1987. 481 U.S. 497.
Procunier v. Martinez. 1974. 416 U.S. 396.
Quinn v. Millsap. 1989. 491 U.S. 95.
R.J. Reynolds v. Durham County. 1986. 479 U.S. 130.
Robertson v. Railroad Labor Board. 1925. 268 U.S. 619.
Roe v. Wade. 1973. 410 U.S. 113.
Tinker v. Des Moines School Dist. 1969. 393 U.S. 503.
Thornburgh v. Abbott. 1989. 490 U.S. 401.
United States v. Fisher. 1805. 6 U.S. (2 Cranch) 358.
United States v. Johnson. 1982. 457 U.S. 537.
United States v. Melvin. 1994. 27 F.3d 703.
United States v. Zolin. 1989. 491 U.S. 554.
Wainwright v. Witt. 1985. 469 U.S. 412.
Washington v. Glucksberg. 1997. 521 U.S. 702.
Witherspoon v. Illinois. 1968. 391 U.S. 510.
Young v. U.S. 1987. 481 U.S. 787.
Youngstown Sheet & Tube Co. v. Sawyer. 1952. 343 U.S. 579.

Index

Note: Page numbers in *italics* indicate figures; those with a *t* indicate tables.

abortion, 5–6, 12
acclimation, of new justices, 30t, 34t, 37t
accommodation. *See* bargaining, among justices
Adams Fruit Co. v. Barrett, 55–57
Adams v. Texas, 60
age, of precedent, 74, 84t, 91t
  lower court compliance and, 86
  multiple concurrences and, 88t
Alito, Samuel, 1, 7
Amendments. *See under* Constitution
anticipatory theory, 87
assisted suicide, 21
attitudinal model, 3–4, 13, 23–24, 42, 121n1
attorney–client privilege, 52, 123n16

Bakke decision, 14–15
bargaining, among justices, 41–70, 45t, 97–98
  successful, 46–59
  unsuccessful, 59–70
Basic v. Levinson, 53–54
Batson v. Kentucky, 61, 66, 124n24
Baum, Lawrence, 12, 76
Benesh, Sara C., 125n8
Berkolow, 6
Blackmun, Harry A., 16–17, 20, 97–98
  on asylum, 18
  bargaining by, 41–70, 45t
  on *Basic v. Levinson*, 53–54

  on *Gray v. Mississippi*, 59–62
  on *Griffith v. Kentucky*, 66–67
  on *Kentucky Dept. of Corrections v. Thompson*, 51
  on *Michigan v. Chesternut*, 67–70
  on *Omni v. Wolff*, 50–51
  on *Pinter v. Dahl*, 48
  on *Quinn v. Millsap*, 57–58
  on *Thornburgh v. Abbott*, 54–55
  on *United States v. Zolin*, 52–53
Blanton v. North Las Vegas, 58–59
Bonneau, Chris W., 125n3
Brennan, William J., Jr., 16, 44, 45t
  on *Basic v. Levinson*, 53–54
  on *Burlington Northern v. Woods*, 49–50
  database on, 43
  on *Mathews v. United States*, 18
  on *Omni v. Wolff*, 51
  on *Pinter v. Dahl*, 48
  types of concurrences by, 31, 32t
Brent, James C., 81
Brown v. Board of Education, 10, 74–75
Burger, Warren Earl, 8, 9t, 24–25
Burlington Northern v. Woods, 49–50

Caldeira, Gregory A., 14, 23, 72
Canons of Judicial Ethics, 95
Carter, Jimmy, 2
case-specific variables, 28–29, 30t, 33, 34t–37t
Celotex Corp. v. Catrett, 63–65

141

Index

censorship, 54–55
Chase, Samuel, 22
Clarke v. Securities Industry Ass'n, 17
Clean Water Act, 62–65
"clear break" exception, 66
collateral review, 66, 124n25
Colorado v. Connelly, 16–17
Commander in Chief Clause, 1–2
complexity of cases, 28, 30t, 33, 34t, 36t, 39, 91t
   lower court compliance and, 86
   See also case-specific variables
compliance. *See* lower court compliance
concurrence model, 31–39, 32t–37t, 97
   lower court compliance and, 77–88, 83t–85t, 88t
   probabilities with, 35–39, 36t–37t, 92t
   results of, 33–35, 34t
   variables in, 26–30, 30t
concurring opinions, 26–39
   acccommodations for, 41–70, 45t
   Canons of Judicial Ethics on, 95
   coding of, 14–16
   dissenting versus, 5–6, 14
   distribution of, 83t
   Frankfurter on, 12
   Ginsburg on, 11
   history of, 22
   impact of, 3–4, 10–14, 41, 71–93, 83t–92t
   by individual justice, 32t
   judicial signaling by, 5–10, *8*, 9t
   lower court compliance and, 73–88, 83t–85t, 88t
   multiple, 87–88, 88t
   policy preferences and, 7–8, 13, 24, 42–43, 75
   proportion of cases with, *8,* 9t, 13, 22
   Roberts on, 13, 121n7
   Scalia on, 11–12, 75
   special, 5, 13, 24–30, 38
   types of, 14–19, 32t, 77–78, 97
   unanimous versus, 10–11, 13, 22, 121n7
   variables in, 26–30, 30t, 34t, 36t–37t, 38–39
Confrontation Clause, 76
Connecticut v. Barrett, 16
Constitution
   First Amendment of, 6–7, 10–11
   Fourth Amendment of, 66–70, 71
   Fifth Amendment of, 19, 54–55
   Sixth Amendment of, 59–60
   Commander in Chief Clause of, 1–2
   Due Process Clause of, 21, 51
   Equal Protection Clause of, 57
   Establishment Clause of, 10–11, 121n5
   Supremacy Clause of, 46–48, 123n8
cooperative relationships, among justices, 27–29, 30t, 33, 34t–37t, 39, 122n5
County of Allegheny v. American Civil Liberties Union, 11
Cover, Albert D., 26
Coy v. Iowa, 75–76
culpability index, 24

Dames & Moore v. Regan, 2
Davis v. Georgia, 59–61
death penalty, 59–60
Diggs v. Owens, 126n12
dissenting opinions, 5–6, 26, 84t, 91t
   Canons of Judicial Ethics on, 95
   effect of, 12–14
   history of, 22
   impact of, 3–4, 79
   multiple concurrences and, 88t
   proportion of cases with, *8,* 9t, 13, 22
   Scalia on, 11
   See also concurring opinions
doctrinal concurrences, 15–16, 90–91, 91t
   distribution of, 83t
   frequency of, 31
   impact of, 77
   by individual justices, 32t
   lower court compliance and, 84–86, 85t

Index

probability of, 35, 36t–37t, 38–39, 92t
regular, 122n7
variables in, 26, 28, 29, 30t, 34t
Doe v. United States, 124n23
driving while intoxicated (DWI), 59, 124n20
Due Process Clause, 21, 51

emphatic concurrences, 15–19, 31, 91t
  distribution of, 83t
  by individual justices, 32t
  lower court compliance and, 85
  probability of, 35, 36t–37t, 39
  variables in, 26, 28, 29, 30t, 34t
endorsement test, 10–11
entrapment, 18
Epstein, Lee, 4, 41–43, 96, 100
Equal Protection Clause, 57–58
Erie analysis, 49
Eskridge, William N., Jr., 125n6
Establishment Clause, 10–11, 121n5
expansive concurrences, 15–16, 31, 90, 91t
  distribution of, 83t
  impact of, 77
  by individual justices, 32t
  lower court compliance and, 84–86, 85t
  probability of, 35, 36t–37t, 39, 92t
  variables in, 26, 30t, 34t

F.C.C. v. Florida Power Corp., 19
Foreign Intelligence Surveillance Act, 1
Frankfurter, Felix, 12
fraud
  attorney-client privilege and, 52, 123n16
  security market, 53–54, 124n17
free speech, 6–7, 121n4
freshmen justices. *See* acclimation, of new justices

Ginsburg, Ruth Bader, 11
good faith allegation, 63–65
Gray v. Mississippi, 59–62

Greenburg, Jan Crawford, 76
Griffith v. Kentucky, 65–67, 125n12
Gruhl, John, 80
Gwaltney v. Chesapeake Bay Foundation, 62–65

Hand, Learned, 87
Hankerson v. North Carolina, 66–67
Hanna v. Plumer, 49, 123n11
Hansford, Thomas G., 72, 81, 89, 125n10, 126n13
Harlan, John Marshall, II, 65–66, 71–72
harmless-error review, 60
Haynie, Stacia L., 23
Head & Armory v. Providence Ins. Co, 122n1
Hubbard, L. Ron, 52

ideologic compatibility, 26–27, 30t, 33, 34t–37t, 91t
  bargaining and, 42–44, 97
  lower court compliance and, 79–81, 84t, 85t, 86–87
  multiple concurrences and, 88t
  probability of, 92t
importance of cases, 28, 30t, 34t, 37t, 80, 91t
  lower court compliance and, 84t
  multiple concurrences and, 88t
  New York Times measure of, 28, 80, 122n6, 125n5
  probability of, 92t
institutional roles, 29–30, 30t, 33–35, 34t
INS v. Cardoza-Fonseca, 18
Iran hostage crisis, 2

Jackson, Robert H., 1–2
Jefferson, Thomas, 11
Johnson, Charles A., 79
Johnson, William, 11
Judicial Common Space score, 79
Judicial Ethics, Canons of, 95
judicial signaling, 5–10, *8*, 9t
Judiciary Act (1925), 23

jury, impartial, 59–60
Justice-Centered Rehnquist Court Database, 21, 28, 29, 31
justice-specific variables, 26–28, 30t, 33, 34t

Katz v. United States, 71–72
Kennedy, Anthony M., 32t, 44, 45t
   on *Blanton v. North Las Vegas*, 59
   on *Michigan v. Chesternut*, 68–70
   on *Morse v. Frederick*, 7
   on *Quinn v. Millsap*, 57–58
   on *United States v. Zolin*, 52–53
Kentucky Dept. of Corrections v. Thompson, 51
Klein, David E., 80
Kluger, Richard, 10, 74
Knight, Jack, 4, 41–43, 100
Kobylka, Joseph F., 96
Kolsky, Meredith, 77
Kyllo v. U.S., 124n1

Lemon v. Kurtzman, 10–11, 121n6
Levinson, Sanford, 1
libel, 80
limiting concurrences, 15–17, 91t
   distribution of, 83t
   impact of, 77–78
   by individual justices, 32t
   lower court compliance and, 85
   probability of, 31, 35–39, 36t–37t
   variables in, 26, 28, 30t, 34t
lower court compliance, 73–88, 83t–85t, 88t

Mackey v. United States, 65–66
Maltzman, Forrest, 4, 13, 41
   on justices' cooperative relationships, 27, 96, 122n5
   on policy accommodations, 43
Marks v. United States, 29
Marshall, John
   bargaining by, 41–70, 45t
   on unanimous opinions, 13, 22, 95
Marshall, Thurgood, 20, 24, 97–98
   on *Adams Fruit Co. v. Barrett*, 56–57
   on *Blanton v. North Las Vegas*, 59
   on *Burlington Northern v. Woods*, 49–50
   on *Gwaltney v. Chesapeake Bay Foundation*, 62–65
   on *Pinter v. Dahl*, 48
   types of concurrences by, 31, 32t
Martinez. See *Procunier v. Martinez*
Maryland v. Craig, 76
Mathews v. United States, 18
Maveety, Nancy, 25
Michigan v. Chesternut, 67–70
Migrant and Seasonal Agricultural Worker Protection Act, 56–57
Miller v. California, 17–18, 122n9
Moorhead, R. Dean, 95–96, 98
Morse v. Frederick, 6
multinomial logit model, 31–33
Murphy, Walter F., 41, 42, 52

narrowest grounds doctrine, 29
negotiating. See bargaining, among justices
net support variable, 87–88
New York Times measure, 28, 80, 122n6, 125n5
noncompliance, 73, 79–81
   See also lower court compliance

O'Brien, David M., 22, 23, 30
obscenity, 122n9
O'Connor, Sandra Day, 27, 45t
   on *Adams Fruit Co. v. Barrett*, 56, 57
   on assisted suicide, 21
   on Confrontation Clause, 76
   endorsement test of, 10–11
   on *Gwaltney v. Chesapeake Bay Foundation*, 63
   on *Omni v. Wolff*, 50–51
   Supremacy Clause and, 46–48
   types of concurrences by, 32t
Omni v. Wolff, 50–51

peremptory challenges, 60–62
Pinter v. Dahl, 48
Pole Attachments Act, 19

policy preferences, 7–8, 13, 24, 42–43, 75
Pope v. Illinois, 17
Powell, Lewis F., Jr., 19, 44, 45t
　on *Burlington Northern v. Woods*, 50
　on *Gray v. Mississippi*, 60–62
　on *Griffth v. Kentucky*, 66–67
　types of concurrences by, 16
precedent, age of, 79, 84t, 91t
　lower court compliance and, 86
　multiple concurrences and, 88t
Procunier v. Martinez, 54–55

Quinn v. Millsap, 57–58
quotas, racial, 76

racial quotas, 76
rape, 75–76
rational-choice model, 24, 42
Ray, Laura Krugman, 5, 6, 15–19
Reddick, Malia, 125n8
Rehnquist, William H., 4, 24, 45t
　on assisted suicide, 21
　on *Blanton v. North Las Vegas*, 59
　concurring opinions and, *8*, 9t, 16, 25–26, 30
　database on, 21, 28, 29, 31
　on judge's task, 6
　on *Kentucky Dept. of Corrections v. Thompson*, 51
　on *Michigan v. Chesternut*, 69
　on *Omni v. Wolff*, 50–51
　on *Thornburgh v. Abbott*, 55
　types of concurrences by, 31, 32t
reluctant concurrences, 17–18, 31, 91t
　distribution of, 83t
　impact of, 77–78
　by individual justices, 32t
　lower court compliance and, 86
　probability of, 35, 36t–37t, 39
　variables in, 26, 30t, 34t
R.J. Reynolds v. Durham County, 46–47
Roberts, John, 6–7, 13, 121n7
Robertson v. Railroad Labor Board, 50–51, 123n15
Roe v. Wade, 5–6

Rules of Decisions Act, 49, 123n12

Scalia, Antonin, 44, 45t, 75
　on *Adams Fruit Co. v. Barrett*, 56–57
　on *Griffth v. Kentucky*, 66–67
　on *Gwaltney v. Chesapeake Bay Foundation*, 63–65
　on *Michigan v. Chesternut*, 67–70
　on obscenity, 17–18
　on *Omni v. Wolff*, 51
　on opinion writing, 11–12
　on *Pinter v. Dahl*, 48
　on *Quinn v. Millsap*, 58
　on Supremacy clause, 46–48
　on *Thornburgh v. Abbott*, 55
　types of concurrences by, 31, 32t
　on *United States v. Zolin*, 52–53
Scientology, 52
search warrants, 71–72
Securities Act (1933), 48
Segal, Jeffrey A., 13, 26, 27
　on attitudinal model, 23–24
　on *Bakke* decision, 14–15
seriatum opinions, 11, 13, 22
sexual abuse, 75–76
Shepard's Citations, 81, 82, 125n8
　reliability of, 125n10, 126n13, 126n19
　strongest letter rule in, 125n11
Spaeth, Harold J., 4, 27, 79, 80
　on attitudinal model, 23–24
　on *Bakke* decision, 14–15
special concurrences, 5, 13, 24–30, 38
Specter, Arlen, 1
Spriggs, James F., II, 72, 75, 81, 89, 125n10, 126n13
stare decisis, 18, 95, 98, 121n2
Stevens, John Paul, 14, 17, 45t
　on *Basic v. Levinson*, 53
　on *Griffth v. Kentucky*, 66–67
　on *Gwaltney v. Chesapeake Bay Foundation*, 62–65
　on *Michigan v. Chesternut*, 69
　on Supremacy Clause, 48
　types of concurrences by, 32t
Stone, Harlan Fiske, 23

strategic model, 4, 13, 24–25
strongest letter rule, 125n11
suicide, assisted, 21

teaching experience, among justices, 30t, 33, 34t–37t, 39
telephone wiretaps, 1, 71–72
Thomas, Clarence, 7
Thornburgh v. Abbott, 54–55
Tinker v. Des Moines Community School Dist., 7, 121n4
Truman, Harry S., 1–2
Turner, Charles C., 25–26

unanimous opinions, 10–11
 Marshall on, 13, 22
 Roberts on, 13, 121n7
United States v. Fisher, 122n2
United States v. Johnson, 66
United States v. Melvin, 126n12
United States v. Zolin, 52–53
University of California at Davis, 14–15
unnecessary concurrences, 19, 31
 distribution of, 83t
 impact of, 78
 by individual justices, 32t
 lower court compliance and, 85
 probability of, 36t–37t, 127n20
 variables in, 30t, 34t

Vietnam War protests, 121n4
visibility, importance and, 80

Wahlbeck, Paul J., 41
Wainwright v. Witt, 60–61
Walker, Thomas G., 13, 22–23
Ward, Artemus, 41
Warren, Earl, *8*, 9t, 10, 74–75
Wasby, Stephen, 79
Washington, Bushrod, 22
Washington v. Glucksberg, 21
Way, Lori Beth, 25–26
Weiden, David L., 41
Westerland, Chad, 27–28, 122n5
White, Byron Raymond, 44, 45t
 on *Adams Fruit Co. v. Barrett*, 56–57
 on *Blanton v. North Las Vegas*, 59
 on *Quinn v. Millsap*, 58
 on *Thornburgh v. Abbott*, 54–55
 types of concurrences by, 16
wiretaps, 1, 71–72
Witherspoon v. Illinois, 59–61
Witkin, B. E., 15, 16, 19
Workers' compensation, 124n18

Youngstown Sheet & Tube Co. v. Sawyer, 1–2
Young v. U.S., 16

Zorn, Christopher J.W., 14, 23, 72